EXPEDITION 196

Expedition 196

A PERSONAL JOURNAL FROM
THE FIRST WOMAN ON RECORD TO TRAVEL
TO EVERY COUNTRY IN THE WORLD

CASSIE DE PECOL

LIONCREST
PUBLISHING

EXPEDITION 196

*A Personal Journal from the First Woman on Record
to Travel to Every Country in the World*

ISBN   978-1-5445-1151-1 *Hardcover*

978-1-5445-1150-4 *Paperback*

978-1-5445-1149-8 *Ebook*

TABLE OF CONTENTS

AUTHOR'S NOTE

To all the women and girls who have dreams of traveling and changing the world, I encourage you to do what has never been done before by any other woman or man, to forge your own path, and to succeed in ways you could have never imagined in order to break the glass ceiling and make women's history.

Men have called me mad; but the question is not yet settled, whether madness is or is not the loftiest intelligence—whether much that is glorious—whether all that is profound—does not spring from disease of thought—from moods of mind exalted at the expense of the general intellect.

—EDGAR ALLAN POE

INTRODUCTION

BEGINNING AT THE END

Everything I'd worked for over the course of the past three years came down to this very moment.

The sound of the rusty steel gates creaking open broke the silence of the twilight hour. I was in the middle of the desert wilderness with nothing but desolate, mountainous terrain to my right and the vast Arabian sea to my left. Camels roamed freely across the horizon, and black-winged kites circled across the sky above. Draped in a black headscarf and wearing baggy black-and-white gypsy pants with a long-sleeved, black, quarter-zipped shirt, I was the only female in sight. I was surrounded by Oman and Yemeni border guards who would dictate every next move I made.

This was my final chance to enter Yemen, the 196th—and final—country I had to visit on what I had termed Expedition 196, my trip around the world. After this, I would claim the Guinness World Record. Yemen was the poorest country in the Middle East and currently under Houthi rebel control. It was certainly not a place where I would be celebrating my achievement with family and friends. In fact, Yemen was the riskiest and most unstable country I had ever entered alone. It was a place that would end up nearly costing me my life.

CHAPTER 1

SEEKING PURPOSE

Live the life of your dreams. Be brave enough
to live the life of your dreams according
to your vision and purpose instead of the
expectations and opinions of others.

—ROY T. BENNETT

My motivation for doing Expedition 196 is both simple and complicated. To know what drove me to undertake this intense, monumental feat of traveling alone to every sovereign nation on earth, is to understand my mind. Thousands of people continue to ask me why and how I accomplished my expedition. They want to know details. Like others who make history, I'm not afraid to be alone. Actually, I prefer it. I don't fear anyone. I'm willing to give my life for it. I don't care about being misunderstood, and it's very difficult to live among the human race when you're not understood, though I am not willing to mold myself into someone I'm not just to fit in. I'm married to the vision I created for myself. I set my own course and am extraordinarily disciplined, determined, serious, and dedicated to accomplishing it. I put in the work and research to know what it would take. A year and a half of planning, plotting courses, getting visas, arranging flights, obtaining sponsors and investors, organizing speaking engagements, and much more. I was ready to go.

The most important lesson I learned on Expedition 196 was this: we are all composed of the same basic makeup. All any human being needs is a hot meal in front of us, a roof over our heads, and someone who loves and supports us. The same is true whether you're Somalian, American, Bolivian, or Middle Eastern; whether you're male or female; and whether you're Muslim or Christian.

The basic needs for human survival connect every single human being on this planet. I'm no better than you, and you're no better than me. Even if you're happier, more financially successful, better looking, or more fulfilled. We are all the same, and we're all in this together.

It's widely known that history makers are mostly misunderstood while they're alive and then celebrated after they're gone. I hope to change that. By sharing the intimate details of the why, you, the reader, might understand the misunderstood and be tolerant and grateful for the lessons.

In seeking purpose, I discovered a lot about myself. From a young age, my brother and I were encouraged to be self-referred, filtering the illusions of the world through our own knowledge. Discovering and learning by a variety of methods, we were homeschooled and experienced Waldorf, Montessori, and public schools. We moved a lot, and each time we settled somewhere different in the same community of towns, Mom would ask if we wanted to be homeschooled or try a different school. We never stopped learning. Even our routines and dreams, our exercise and food choices, our conversations and travels, and our typical ups and downs were subjects for discussions and opportunities to learn. I thought her question was wonderful. I could never sit still in one place and loved getting a taste of new forms of education.

My yearning to explore new forms of education and places led me to attend college in different states and countries. I didn't graduate. Instead, I dropped out a semester short of graduation. Much of my self-education as a young adult came from living the motto: "fake it till you make it." You know, the English aphorism suggesting if you imitate competence and confidence, you'll eventually realize these same qualities in your life. I was able to live in nine countries and travel to twenty-five altogether between the ages of twenty-one and twenty-three by following this motto.

I was always purpose driven. There had to be a reason

for, and purpose to, whatever I was doing. As a child, I wanted to be a storm chaser and meteorologist. I wasn't good at math and science, so no matter how hard I tried, it became clear this wasn't going to be my path. I wasn't willing to be committed enough to do what it took to make it happen. My purpose wasn't going to be wife, mother, and stability because comfort wasn't my thing. Knowing and realizing as a teen that my mind and thoughts weren't normal, my life wouldn't be normal either. I had panic attacks, depression, and bouts of anxiety. I hid them well and wasn't going to worry my parents about something they probably couldn't help with anyway. I remember thinking, later on, while babysitting for a living, that I'd better create an important, lucrative career for myself by age thirty, or I'd take my own life. An extreme thought, I know. Interestingly, these thoughts pushed me to make human history.

I had discovered that I was an introvert, even though people saw me as an extrovert. I learned about the concept of the "alpha female" and believed myself to be just that. I was fascinated by what I learned about ants. I was a visual learner and communicator and, to this day, prefer to correspond more through email than phone calls. I knew by this time, I was driven, self-reliant, had a mighty will, and was impatient. By this time, I was just twenty-two.

ANTS AMONG US

As a young adult, I had visions of being the female version of Anthony Bourdain or innovator Richard Branson. They are "bullet ants."

Prior to Expedition 196, I spent four months living in both the Ecuadorian and Bolivian Amazon and surviving twenty-one days naked in the Panamanian jungle. During this time, I tasted many different variations of ants.

I started to pay close attention to the ants that were thriving all around me when I lived deep within the Amazon jungle. On one specific occasion, I remember walking through the jungle with the leaves crunching beneath my feet. Warm rain poured, watering the flora that existed below the soft, muddy surface and amidst the trees. The air was sticky and humid. I wore a face net to protect myself from the mosquitoes buzzing around my head. The complex smells alone made the trek so worth it.

The first ants that I noticed were the obvious big black ones. They stood out to me not only because of their size but also because they had the power to inflict immense pain upon even a relative giant, like myself, with their sting. The bullet ants, also known as *Paraponera clavata*, are particularly formidable. They thrive because they are able to successfully fend off any enemy, including humans.

As I examined those bullet ants, I thought to myself, "I want to be the human version of *that* in our kingdom." For me, those bullet ants represented people I looked up to, as mentioned earlier, like the innovator Richard Branson, or United Nations Secretary-General Ban Ki-moon, aviation pioneer Amelia Earhart, and philanthropists like Leonardo DiCaprio and Oprah Winfrey. In my mind, the bullet ant represented the person who facilitates massive global change, makes big bucks, and inspires billions of people in their own lives. They are the bullet ant equivalent of the people in our history books who positively shape the way our future unfolds.

Upon closer observation, I noticed run-of-the-mill black and reddish ants scattering above and between the clumps of dirt. While the reddish ones stung a bit, they weren't anything to fear. They loved working together to build their colonies, to transfer pieces of food to one another down the line, and to march to the beat of the same drum. Their species wouldn't be able to thrive without the cohesion of teamwork. As I looked at them, I realized I would never want to be one of those ants due to my difficulty working with others and following the crowd.

Then, finally, there were the tiny lemon ants, or *Myrmelachista schumanni*. One day, a man who lived in a local Achuar community (an indigenous community made up of around eighteen thousand individuals) named Yantu (which translates to "moon") led me to a giant tree. He hacked a bit of bark from the tree, revealing hundreds of tiny, fragile ants. He handed me a few of them and said, "Eat!" Reluctantly, I chucked the little things in my mouth and *pop*! A juicy, lemony zing immediately coated the inside of my mouth!

"Lemon ants!" Yantu said.

These ants represent the small but mighty. They like to live where there is little to no bio diversity, compared to the surrounding area, and they inject formic acid into plants. This injection causes the plants to die within twenty-four hours. Though not blatantly visible to the naked eye, like the bullet ants or traditional ants, the lemon ants make the greatest impact on the living flora around them, and they're unexpectedly sweet.

As I pondered the characteristics and pecking order of ants, I came to the realization that three prototypes of humans also make our planet what it is. To this day, I strive to become that bullet ant. However, the longer I thrive and survive, the more I notice my tendencies relate more closely to that of a lemon ant. Though I'm not noticed to the degree of my idols because I'm smaller, I *have* been able to make one specific and substantial impact in the travel industry. I might look sweet on the outside, but my willpower and perseverance have allowed me to have a far more profound effect on humanity in the field of travel than one might expect at a glance. I've made history and paved the way for future men, and especially women, who choose to travel to every country in the world.

A CEO AT TWENTY-ONE

For all of the ways we are the same, there are also many ways in which my thoughts and actions differ greatly from those of the average person.

I often visualize myself looking down at earth from the perspective of the universe. From this vantage point, I am able to perceive how small earth truly is and, more importantly, how small people are. From this vantage point, humans really do look like ants. Looking at both our planet and human beings through this lens makes traveling to even the most dangerous of countries feel like home. Wherever I might be in the world, I realize that we're more alike than we are different. The media likes to make us scared of one another and of certain places, but once we realize how much we all have in common (and that none of us are here for that long anyway), those fears turn to dust.

My first year of college in Costa Rica, my teachers became frustrated because I didn't learn like the other kids. I preferred to focus on my own independent work and projects.

Moving on, after I took various international internships, I volunteered for USAID as a marketing and sustainability advisor for small tour companies. I did this in the Bolivian Amazonian town of Rurrenabaque. Applicants for this particular internship were required to have a bachelor's and be working towards their master's. I had neither. They accepted me because they liked and respected what they read, saw, and knew was my passion for this work. Being accepted into this program was a career milestone. Working closely alongside two other interns, it struck me that I'd always somehow known since age thirteen. My undiagnosed anxiety and depression led me to isolate myself as much as possible. This in turn hindered the teamwork required to complete our projects. Over the course of the internship, I did my work alone. While the others worked together, I tried my very best to do the work that was asked of me. There were certain things at the time that I didn't understand until much later in life. Isolating myself from the team made them not want to work with me, and it made me not want to accept their help. To make matters worse at that time, my grandpa died, and I couldn't get back for the funeral.

I had aspirations of becoming a successful entrepreneur. I set up an LLC, poured what little money I had into a professional website, and created a portfolio that positioned me as a "sustainability consultant." In college, I had double-majored in environmental studies and global studies. Combined with the three and a half years I spent googling my way through a business education, I was confident that I had enough knowledge to advise luxury hotels around the world on how to optimize revenues by increasing their energy efficiency and sustainability initiatives. This was 2010, and I firmly believed tourism was shifting in the direction of sustainable travel. I thought that even your average luxury traveler would be more apt to stay at a sustainable resort than a Sandals, even if they only chose to sit on the beach and sip margaritas.

In addition to my website and portfolio, I built an online blog and made money through article submissions. I built my résumé while traveling in this way, as well as working for free at hotels around the world in exchange for room and board. This is how I traveled to twenty-five countries in roughly two and a half years.

The life of a travel blogger suited me. Unfortunately, it wasn't financially fruitful enough to sustain world travels. To be honest, I also wanted to experience making real money through a typical nine-to-five job like all my friends were doing. What also had me delve into the workaday world was the fact that I was influenced by people telling me over and over again that I was naive for failing to see all that my own country had to offer. Also, people perceived the world as a dangerous place and thought me a fool for wanting to go to the Middle East, a goal of mine for years.

Borne out of anger, intense drive, and a passion to prove the naysayers wrong, I drove across America many times and experienced forty-six of the fifty states. While they were beautiful and full experiences, I still craved international travel. I couldn't see the United States ever being my favorite country. Little did I know.

FROM NINE-TO-FIVE TO *NAKED AND AFRAID*

Being a nomadic traveler as a career wasn't looked highly upon at the time. I endured a nine-to-five job for six months. It would come up in conversation down the line, and all I could say was, "I tried that." It was a sales job that was terrible in every way but one. I had steady money coming in for the first time, which meant I could go out for a meal now and again. It also meant I could afford my hobby of half-Ironman racing. Renting a bike for the race and buying used equipment and necessary clothes meant I could stay in shape and be healthy while living the life of a nine-to-fiver.

I shared a two-bedroom with a male roommate, and we barely communicated. My room had a blow-up mattress borrowed from a friend, one sheet set, a suitcase, my mom's Bianchi road bike that she'd had for years, which was passed down to her from a friend, and a large map of the world tacked to the wall. That's it. I didn't have much. I didn't need much, although I craved much more out of life than I was living.

One evening, after five business owners spat at me in a single day as I tried to sell them the one phone service I was working for, I sat in front of the TV with a glass of Two Buck Chuck from Trader Joes. I rarely watched TV. I found myself staring blankly as a couple of naked people ran through the jungle. It was a show on Discovery channel that was funny yet baffling. At the end of the show, viewers were encouraged to fill out a casting application in order to be on the show themselves.

Sick of my job and feeling like I had no way out, I decided to give it a shot. I grabbed my HP laptop and perched it on the arm of the couch. I applied as I continued watching this weird TV show. Days later, I received a call from a woman telling me that my application was being considered. A few weeks later, I was flown out to LA for the in-person interview. I couldn't believe how quickly this was moving along. The fact that I'd potentially be on TV was, I'll admit, exciting. "Maybe," I thought, "things are looking up."

The show was called *Naked and Afraid*. It was a survival show that paired together a man and a woman who didn't know each other. These pairs were then placed in the middle of a remote wilderness environment with one tool each. They had to survive naked for twenty-one days. At the time, I had nothing to lose.

When I was homeschooled as a child, an outdoor expert

named Scott came to our house once a week every week for a year to teach my brother and me wilderness survival skills. In the winter, we'd go out to the backyard in nature and make igloos, which we'd call home for the day. If we were feeling daring, then we'd stay there for the night. In the spring, we learned how to collect rainfall for water and how to forage for mushrooms and fiddleheads to make a salad for lunch. In the summer, we were taught how to create friction fires and shelters made of twigs and ferns. And in the fall, we went caving and made massive leaf piles, all while trying to avoid the nasty ticks that were part of the New England landscape we grew up in. The idea was to survive in the wilderness with basic skills, and we learned to be outside from 8:00 a.m. to 8:00 p.m. in all kinds of weather.

For a year of my university education, I attended Green Mountain College in Vermont, where I took a liking to weekend camping trips and whitewater kayaking using a rolling technique. I'll always remember when one of the female seniors and trip leaders made fun of me for bringing a pink camera that my Mom had bought for me to document my trip. I always secluded myself from the group to allow my senses to be engulfed in nature's sounds and sights.

Given my brief background in wilderness survival and more general experiences in the outdoors, I convinced myself that I had what it took to at least attempt to survive twenty-one days naked and afraid. Deep down, I knew that the greatest challenge was not survival but managing to work toward a common goal as a team.

The producers thought I had what it took too. I was cast. While the challenge itself was great, I was disappointed to learn how scripted and edited reality television is. For the first ten days, I was the only woman on set, surrounded by male producers, cinematographers, sound editors, photographers, my partner, and local indigenous men.

Halfway through the twenty-one-day challenge, my teammate Forrest and I, who were already struggling to get along, met up with two other team members in a *Naked and Afraid: Double Jeopardy* special. Up until that point, Forrest and I were maintaining the shelter together. He was in charge of collecting oranges and spearing fish. I crafted our water source, made our shoes for the journey ahead, collected coconuts, and attempted to start a friction fire to cook our meat despite soggy wood and sporadic rainfall. In the end, neither of us were able to light a fire, even though we both had experience doing so in the past. Though we didn't get along at times, we worked as a team, utilizing one another's skills to get by for the first ten days.

When the other team of two appeared, I knew this was

going to be the most challenging experience of my life, working as a team of four to survive for ten days straight, no break. Four naked adults, one four-by-three-foot shelter, sleep deprivation, starvation, dehydration, sickness, rain, and cold air temperatures, all provided the perfect reality TV backdrop for bickering, vulnerability, and failure.

While I was happy to finally have a woman to communicate with, we were nonetheless strangers, and we were both depleted by that point. My female partner, Manu, and I worked together to collect vines, leaves, and twigs to create our shelter. Then we began to focus on our strengths in order to survive as a group. Manu continued to tame the shelter, while Forrest (my original partner) took to the ocean to spear fish. Russell, Manu's partner, focused on our water source, and I collected nibbles, such as snails, from the river and berries that had fallen to the ground from the monkeys shuffling the leaves above. We all took turns adding to the shelter, foraging meals, collecting water from the seep in coconut bowls that we made, going to the bathroom in the ocean and then drying off in the sun afterwards (which most viewers assumed was "tanning"), and building supplies for our extraction day.

Toward the last few days of our time together, I began to feel more isolated from the group, and started performing responsibilities and tasks on my own. One notable instance was when the group was working on the raft. While I also worked on the raft, though not as much, the editors chose not to add that footage in, which made me look like a useless character. Little did anyone know that, meanwhile, I was building oars to get us out to sea!

While I wasn't a wilderness survivalist by career, I tried my very best. Moments of that experience brought me back to the times when I was made fun of in high school and college simply for being who I was. Because I was a novice survivalist and a young blonde woman, I was immediately pegged as the bitchy character. I was also given less respect by my peers because of my lack of survival knowledge and inability to work in a team setting.

With the film rolling, producers would ask questions like, "How did that snail taste?"

"Well," I would reply, "I was grateful to have a snail to eat."

"But how did it *taste?*" they would press.

"It was okay. But again, I was grateful to have one."

Still, the producers would push on. "Explain the texture. Was it crunchy? Salty?"

"Yes, it was crunchy and salty," I would repeat.

They would then abandon the pretense of an interview and tell me to say, "The snail was disgusting. It was crunchy and salty, and I didn't like it."

Through this reality television form of interrogation, my answers somehow went from something as innocuous as, "I was grateful just to have a piece of food," to mean and ungrateful responses. Lines like this added to the drama and to the character I was intended to portray. And trust me, we each had a character, and all of us were disappointed by how that character was portrayed at times.

Ultimately, those twenty-one days ended up being both the best and worst experience of my life up until that point in time. They allowed me to come to terms with how isolated I really was in my head. Little did I know, the mental torture was still to come immediately following the premiere of our episode. Online, viewers and critics alike were ruthless. My inbox and social media platforms were flooded with everything from degrading comments to hate speech to death threats. To this day, I know when our episode is rerun thanks to the hate messages waiting to greet me in my inbox.

Being who I was, or at least who the producers painted me to be on television, was the ultimate exposure. I knew from the beginning that going on TV naked would ruin me in some way, but, at the time, I had nothing to lose.

What was more concerning though was that it took an experience like this to make me come to terms with my dark thoughts and views on life.

After *Naked and Afraid*, I was finally able to fully accept the fact that my suicidal thoughts and isolation from others was not normal. I realized that something was wrong within my mind. Still, I was afraid to seek help because, deep down, I knew that in order to heal myself, I would have to succeed in my career. All my life experiences up to and very much including that point reinforced the fact that I must walk this earth alone. Which, of course, is precisely what I did in the most literal sense.

I used the cash from *Naked and Afraid* to pay off some bills, lease a car, and run away to LA in hopes of potentially capitalizing on the exposure. What a failure that was! What was I thinking?

I ended up snagging a studio apartment at the top of Lake Arrowhead for $950 per month. The village was perched at a roughly 5,000-foot elevation, and it was a three-hour drive away from one of my two babysitting jobs in Woodland Hills, California. I worked weekends at another babysitting job in the Pacific Palisades, which was yet another four- or five-hour round trip drive from my apartment up in the mountains. I spent approximately eighty-five hours every week babysitting and commuting back and forth just to financially stay afloat. All of this was the result of yet another fake-it-till-you-make-it scenario. I didn't tell my employers where I lived for fear they wouldn't give me the job. Jobs were hard to come by. For months, I made this five-hour commute every day.

Finally, after all this time, I was able to afford a studio apartment in Calabasas, which was much closer to my jobs. After a few months of living this chaotic, busy LA lifestyle, I purchased seven entrepreneurial books and read them all within one month. For someone who isn't a reader, this was an extremely important turning point for me.

I now knew, once and for all, I didn't fit into life as a regular, typical, colonized ant. It was time to become the bullet ant that I had envisioned myself to be.

CHAPTER 2

THE BIRTH OF EXPEDITION 196

*Every journey taken always includes the path not
taken, the detour through hell, the crossroads
of indecision and the long way home.*

—SHANNON L. ALDER

Following a lot of deliberation about what to do with
my life and career, in the spring of 2014, I decided, "I'm
going to space." Since my lack of math and science skills
wouldn't allow me to do *exactly* that, I decided to do the
next best thing. I vowed to devote myself to building a
career around travel in a way no other woman had ever
done before. I decided to travel to every country in the
world alone. This, I thought, would surely upgrade my
status from a regular ant to a bullet ant.

I established Expedition 196 with the goal of positively

enhancing our world, creating a flourishing career for myself, and facing death up close and personal. The flame was fueled by two fires. First, by my own personal feelings of unworthiness. And second, by how minuscule I felt compared to the Richard Bransons and Nelson Mandelas of our world. It was time for me to take flight and risk my life in order to succeed in the career and life that I desired.

Initially, I thought it would take two months to plan out my great adventure. In the end, the physical and mental planning of Expedition 196 actually took one-and-a-half years. As a woman traveling alone, I took it upon myself to register for Krav Maga, an Israeli practical self-defense practice. Within eighteen months, I reached level two, which enabled me to actually defend myself should a life-threatening situation present itself.

Los Angeles, California. Photo by Photek Films

COMMITTING MYSELF TO MY GREATEST ENDEAVOR

To secure sponsorship for my expedition, companies had to have a reason to invest in me. At face value, a twenty-six-year-old, blonde American woman traveling alone to places like North Korea and Syria is not the smartest investment for a company to make. Proving myself and my commitment to my expedition and business venture required developing a firm and tangible goal. I did this in the form of a Guinness World Record.

Upon researching the Guinness database, the travel record that seemed most applicable was "Fastest Time to Visit all Sovereign Countries." Only one person had set this record at the time, and it was a man. It was then that I saw a great window of opportunity to be the first female to break the record, which would also make me the first woman on public record to travel to every sovereign country in the world.

This record required that I step foot into 193 sovereign nations, the Vatican (a nonmember observer state), and Taipei, the latter of which, according to Guinness, does not have member status but is, nonetheless, effectively sovereign. If you're doing the math, this actually equals a total of 195 countries. Even though I ended up traveling to more than 195 countries over the course of my expedition (somewhere around 210 if you count dependencies, territories, and colonies like St. John and Reunion Island), I dubbed my trip Expedition 196. I settled on 196 because I also intended to travel to Kosovo, a disputed territory and partially recognized state.

Calabasas, California

Setting or breaking a Guinness World Record is no joke. It requires following a substantial set of rules in order to officially make the Guinness World Records. There is a long wait once a person applies for the record they wish to set. In my case, it took about four months to find out whether I qualified to break this record. Once you hear back, you're then given a downloadable packet specific to the record you intend to break. This packet outlines the rules and regulations that must be met in order to set your record.

For my specific record, I had to collect copious amounts of evidence. At times, I risked my life to obtain this evidence. Evidence included things like signed witness statements, photographs, videos, passport stamps, GPS coordinates to track exact locations, credit and debit card transactions, phone logs, and transportation and accommodation receipts, to name just a few. Each country I visited required four solid pieces of proof for submission. I also had to pass through border control in each country in order to officially enter.

Once inside of a country, there was no requirement for the amount of time I had to stay; however, I was not to exceed more than fourteen days at a time in any country, no matter how badly I wanted to hang around and soak it in. This fourteen-day limit included "breaks." Breaks were considered an official pause in the journey. This might mean flying back home and partaking in private transport, like driving a car. But even these breaks were to be no longer than fourteen days. Also of note is that the days during which I took a pause would still add to my overall time for my record attempt.

I was allowed only to take "scheduled, public transport" in the form of planes, trains, ferries, and busses. Taxis were allowed, but for no more than thirty miles total within a country. This rule in and of itself really limited my ability to dive into the sort of off-the-beaten-track locations that I had become so accustomed to exploring.

It probably goes without saying that figuring out how my expedition would be structured in order to meet the requirements for Guinness World Records ended up taking a lot of planning.

KIDNAP AND RANSOM INSURANCE?

I had to file an LLC and open new bank accounts for the funding I obtained specifically for the expedition, which was, by this point, a legitimate business. I had to launch and update social media accounts for Expedition 196 on a daily basis, including Facebook, Twitter, YouTube, Instagram, and Snapchat. I created a promo video for the expedition, which required tons of B-roll and professional footage. I had to develop both my personal and expedition websites, both of which I designed and developed on my own.

Then came the "team." By this point, it probably won't surprise you to hear that this time around, my team was a virtual one, and it worked well. Once again relying on my fake-it-till-you-make-it skills, I obtained supporters who agreed to have their names and likenesses listed on my website to demonstrate to other organizations that I had a great "support team." This support team included "The World's Greatest Living Explorer" and multiple Guinness World Record holder Ranulph Fiennes; *Into the Cold* filmmaker (and also Orlando Bloom's cousin) Sebastian Copeland; actor and director Paul Lieberstein of *The Office*; and high school friend and ninja on NBC's *American Ninja Warrior*, Joe Moravsky; among others. With that in place, I reached out to nonprofits for endorsement and companies for sponsorship.

Securing the funds and finding an organization that would support my dream turned out to be the biggest challenge of the entire expedition. Days turned to night, and my fingers started to hurt as I spent hours on end sending out thousands of emails to various organizations, including my pitch, sponsorship deck, and proposal. Initially, my core mission was to promote women's rights in every country; however, I quickly realized that women's activism could potentially land me in life-threating scenarios in places like Iran and North Korea, so I figured I'd leave that to the professionals—or at least women who are educated in the field.

Then, I thought I'd promote sustainability. Again, I quickly came to realize that the gruesome amount of public transportation I would have to take for the Guinness Record attempt would wreak havoc on my carbon footprint. World peace was a tangible mission I knew most people could get behind, so I stuck with that as my core mission.

Nonetheless, my conscience wouldn't let me look away from my passion for sustainability and, specifically, for responsible tourism. I decided to plant as many trees as I could to offset my carbon footprint, stay in as many sustainable hotels as possible, educate the youth around the world about how to travel responsibly, and volunteer for a nonprofit organization called Adventure Scientists by collecting water samples from waterways around the world. These samples were then sent to labs and tested for the presence of micro plastics.

With my LLC filed, team secured, and mission solidified, it was time to find a nonprofit to endorse my expedition. More importantly, I needed an organization that would believe in me enough to provide assistance and connections around the world. Day after day, I was turned down by nonprofit organizations because I did not hold a college degree. The lack of a college degree really limited me. To this day, I don't regret not finishing. In fact, it ultimately made the reward feel that much sweeter when I finally identified two nonprofit organizations that were interested in endorsing my expedition.

Although neither of these organizations offered financial assistance, the founder of the International Institute for Peace through Tourism (IIPT) took a liking to my cause and offered to connect me to Skål International. Skål is a professional organization of tourism leaders around the world that promotes global tourism and friendship across all branches of the travel and tourism industry. Skål, in turn, connected me with the United Nations secretary general for tourism, who networked me to various ministers of tourism and mayors throughout the world. These political figures invited me to conferences to network and secure funding. They also helped organize tree plantings and keynote sessions with students.

Pitching myself to potential investors brought me back to my days of *Naked and Afraid*, but instead of feeling vulnerable and at the mercy of the environment, I felt vulnerable and at the mercy of big CEOs. I created business cards and pamphlets to showcase my efforts and attended event after event, throwing myself out there in a world that I really knew little of. LinkedIn was a great resource for honing in on potential investors. It allowed me to connect with CEOs, CMOs, CBOs, and other executives so I could convince them that their company would benefit by investing cash, goods, or services into the expedition. From Clif Bar to Air New Zealand to AIG and Krav Maga Worldwide, I was able to secure a good dozen sponsors prior to departing on my expedition.

One of my sponsors was a satellite GPS company that promised to provide a reliable mode of communication I could depend on, both for my own safety and for Guinness tracking purposes. This GPS was particularly crucial in more precarious areas where there was either a lot of wilderness or political uncertainty. Unfortunately, I don't believe this device was tested in some areas, as it failed to provide a signal in most of Africa, the Pacific islands, and the Middle East. In the end, I was alone and untraceable by GPS in many countries throughout Africa, the Pacific and Indian Islands, and Asia. Since this device was also meant to clock a good deal of my Guinness proof, I had to use other means to document my location, such as my iPhone. Not surprisingly, mobile phone signals were also sparse.

With my sponsors in place, now I had to actually *plan* the trip. Given my tendency to work best alone and my independent nature, I decided to plan everything by myself. I bought a map, put it on the wall, and began mapping out every leg of my trip, accounting for hotels, visas, weather patterns, and political rallies so as to avoid potential cancellations and delays.

Thanks to AIG, I was able to secure not only travel and health insurance but also kidnap and ransom insurance. The latter two were necessary for my parents to be able to sleep at night. AIG enabled me to be well equipped not only with insurance but also with resources and knowledge about what to do, where to go, and who to call should I find myself in a life-threatening situation. Speaking of life-threating situations, I had to apply for as many visas as possible in advance in order to avoid problems at border control. This required obtaining a second passport.

Finally, I needed to not just learn but *master* a DSLR. This camera allowed me to serve as my own one-man camera crew, filming every step of the expedition for my documentary. I also journaled every single day from the very beginning of this process in order to write the very book you have in your hands right now.

CHAPTER 3

SPEED

People would rather live in a community
with unreasonable claims than face
loneliness with their truth.

—BANGAMBIKI HABYARIMANA

Imagine running a virtual race in ninety-five-degree heat and 80 percent humidity on the island of Phuket in Thailand. How can a human speed through 196 countries whilst also speeding within each country? More importantly, *why* would someone do that?

Many people don't understand that achieving a Guinness World Record involves much more than sending an email to the organization to notify them about what you've accomplished. The entire process is very regimented and steeped in rules and regulations. Quite honestly, this made for a very tiresome and unenjoyable experience.

WHY TRAVEL FOR SPEED?

So, why did I choose to rush through the landmasses and cultures that comprise our world? Many people are confused about why I would travel to every country in the world so quickly. Wouldn't it be better to take the time to enjoy myself and the unique experience each country offered? In many ways, the answer is yes. But there are a few reasons why I chose to speed through 196 countries.

Most importantly, I saw the imminent and unavoidable path to my demise as plain as day. From a young age, I came to terms with the fact that my life could end in a moment's time. For some reason, I became obsessed with death and the whys and hows of it. I witnessed my aunt's passing at a young age when I was in middle school. In the ensuing years, I read or heard about celebrity deaths and the deaths of my friends' grandparents, and then their parents. Then a friend died, which not only made death seem all too real but also made me understand that the amount of time I had was unknown.

I never understood why people planned for the future when there was no guarantee of it. One thing I did know was my chances of dying of something—cancer, dementia, a car accident, etc.—would only increase as I got older. You know when people say things like, "Live each day as if it were your last" or "Take advantage of your young years?" Well, I took those words to heart, even as I saw so many people around me doing the opposite.

In high school, I experienced panic attacks as a result of thinking that I was dying. My parents, brother, and I figured I was a hypochondriac. The panic attacks lessened as I got older, but the anxiety and depression didn't. My parents don't even know this, but when I was in high school, I thought I would be the cause of my own demise, and that terrified me. Thoughts like this were what later made me come to terms with the possibility that I had depression, even though the thought of depression terrified me then and still does to this day. I didn't think I'd live past thirty or have the opportunity to see the world slowly, at my own pace.

Thankfully, in the course of the eight years I spent traveling both America and the world, I had already gotten the travel bug mostly out of my system. Now it was time to get serious about my career. I was sick of being broke. I hadn't found my place in the sun like all of my friends had. I was sick of backpacking and not making any money from what I loved to do. Most importantly, I still was striving to be a bullet ant and to make a massive and significant positive change on our world, while also becoming financially successful.

My career goal was to be the next Samantha Brown, to

have my own travel-oriented TV show and successful nonprofit organization to enhance the world. These goals were not going to happen without committing to a business and being driven enough to see my next big project through to its end.

All of the projects I'd started before Expedition 196—from my blog to my consultancy business to babysitting to *Naked and Afraid*—led me to this moment. In my eyes, this was my last chance at life, my last chance to experience all the world has to offer and to make something of myself from it all.

Yes, I was traveling to beat the clock, but I also made an effort to see or do one thing in each country and to speak to one person to learn their story during my visit. While I was able to gain a new experience and knowledge from each country, I nonetheless felt jaded and disgruntled most of the time. The combination of my responsibilities and yearning to engage in experiences often meant I would go anywhere from twenty-four to sixty-three hours without sleep.

Despite my constant rush, I was still able to experience breathing in the air and stomping on the ground of 196 different countries, communicating with people from 196 countries, and planting trees all over the world, all while building my business and making lifelong friendships. All of this was worth every compacted moment.

I will never be able to explain to you exactly what I experienced or endured in each of the 196 countries, simply because I don't want to, those experiences have shaped who I am, and that's the joy of traveling alone. You collect a series of magical experiences all for yourself. I am different than I was before as a direct result of every conversation, every student I met and took selfies with, every hour of every day that was devoted to growing my business and making a greater impact, every panic attack and moment of self-growth. None of this is to mention the responsibility and education I committed myself to, both for the year and a half prior to the expedition and for the eighteen months and ten days of travel.

Even without the benefit of a lot of time, I still learned what places I liked and which ones I didn't. I tasted food from every country. And most importantly, I learned one human being's story in every country about why and how they chose to thrive instead of just survive.

There was another benefit to these short visits as well. I didn't have the time to build up fear far in advance of traveling to either the lesser-known or more precarious nations, or to spend copious amounts of time in places where I didn't feel comfortable. Instead, I was able to walk in to new places with a completely open mind, leaving all my preconceptions at the door. I was able to embrace new moments.

Whereas most travelers are fearful of traveling to places like North Korea or Somalia, I quickly learned we're all just the same. People are the same and, believe it or not, so are our basic ways of life. Knowing this, I would go back to any of these 196 countries in a heartbeat. However, it took me traveling quickly to fully comprehend the value of life and sameness of human creatures.

It's also noteworthy that I traveled during the 2016 US presidential elections. Not having much of a passion for politics myself, I let the world teach me who to vote for. I couldn't *not* hear what they had to say. So I listened and I learned. I did this in Libya, Honduras, the Congo, Brunei, Tuvalu, and everywhere in-between.

Finally, in places like Nauru and South Sudan, I had to be cautious about how long I could stay. These and some other countries only had incoming and outgoing flights once a week. Hotels were very expensive and were often few and far between. Forget about hostels—they were non-existent. I was often faced with the decision of whether to spend $1,000 for a one-week stay or to not stay overnight at all, instead just paying for the round-trip flight in and out of the country. Because of my limited time frame and undependable budget, I often had no other choice than the latter.

EQUAL GENDERS, UNEQUAL TIME

Roughly five months into my record attempt, Guinness contacted me to let me know they were separating the record into two categories: male and female. With this, they were giving men three years to break the standing record and women four years. This really bothered me. I couldn't understand why women required more time to step onto an airplane. It seemed so unequal and made no sense whatsoever.

In the course of this conversation, Guinness mentioned that two other women who were also attempting to break the record had told them that visiting Saudi Arabia was nearly impossible for females. My expedition was already garnering media attention at that point, especially throughout travel Facebook groups, and I have a feeling these other women saw my feat and wanted to challenge me for it. The problem was they had only visited a few countries and apparently didn't know what they were talking about when it came to Saudi Arabia since they hadn't yet traveled there. Having already visited Saudi Arabia on my own by that point, I was disappointed because it was clear to me that Guinness hadn't put as much research into Saudi Arabia as I had. Neither had these two women, apparently. Saudi Arabia was actually one of the easier visas to obtain in the course of my travels. As a US citizen, the only option is to apply for a business visa, and with my LLC, that was easy enough. So this told me these women were not only wrong but must have been trying to cheat their way around the world by claiming that women "needed more time" to obtain visas for places like Saudi Arabia, which simply isn't accurate.

Among the many stresses that came with this record attempt—with speed being the greatest—perhaps it wasn't surprising that these women approached Guinness to increase the record time limit. Nonetheless, it just seemed wrong to me, and I felt that rather than moving us closer to gender equality, it moved us in the wrong direction. Either way, I was able to communicate this to Guinness, and they decided the best way to handle the situation was to have two separate records: fastest time and fastest male/female.

Riyadh, Saudi Arabia

MY DAILY GRIND

Speed was a concern not only in terms of how quickly I could get from place to place but also in terms of getting things done. In general, travel can be all-encompassing, but it is particularly so when you're traveling for the purposes of achieving a record or for business. I lost twenty pounds in eighteen months and ten days because food was the last thing on my mind. I was constantly anxiety-ridden from my massive workload, which involved not only the record, but also my career. The stress left my throat feeling constricted to the point where eating felt like a chore. All my senses were on overdrive because of fear, exhilaration, time pressure, and my desire to be the best and to effect great change in a finite period of time.

On average, I dedicated fifteen hours of every day I traveled to my computer. This included emails to continue to secure funding and sponsors, editing vlogs, organizing my next speaking engagements and meetings, updating my PowerPoint presentation, backing up all data on external hard drives, submitting visa applications, updating my websites and social media, planning my next day of travel, communicating with family back home, logging proof for Guinness, journaling, communicating with Adventure Scientists to ensure they'd received my micro plastics samples, uploading my footage for the documentary, gaining inspiration for social media photos, editing the photos I took, researching places to go (or to *not* go) in the next country, and more.

Every day for 558 days, my schedule looked something like this: I would get up at 4:00 a.m., walk, run, lift, type, explore, have meetings, speak at various engagements, plant trees, film, create, publish, sleep, and repeat, all before falling into bed again at 10:00 p.m. Of course, depending upon travel, my schedule varied greatly, but the general day-to-day duties remained the same.

CHAPTER 4

FEAR, RISK, AND THE UNKNOWN

PERU, YEMEN, AND TUNISIA

Let fear be your fire to fuel your greatest embers within and achieve the unimaginable.

—CASSIE DE PECOL

Fear is a healthy response to situations of physical, emotional, and mental dangers. It's an unpleasant emotion and one that I felt almost daily on my expedition. A few notable moments come to mind immediately.

There is risk in anything we do that takes us out of our comfort zone. Taking a chance invites risk of ridicule, peril, hazards, and probabilities of all kinds of negative circumstances. Risks, by their very nature, mean things may not turn out as we had planned. On the other hand, taking risks mean you have the chance to do what other people think is impossible. I did.

The unknown, by its very definition, means the unexplored, the mysterious, the far away and exotic, the distant, and the undiscovered. These words all perfectly describe my experiences throughout Expedition 196.

PERU

It was 9:00 p.m. when I fetched a taxi to Jorge Chávez International Airport in Lima, Peru. Even in Peru, taxi drivers are equipped with Waze, which, to my unfortunate surprise, took us through back alley roads in order to avoid the heavy, rush-hour traffic. As we drove, I thought to myself, "What a sketchy area. I wouldn't want to be caught walking around here alone at night."

We came to a stop at a traffic light. All of a sudden, a young boy no more than fourteen years old banged on the driver's side window with his fist. I quickly realized he was armed with knives and a gun, which hung from the side of his belt. Both front windows were rolled down about two inches, but the back windows were completely raised shut.

At first, I thought the boy was trying to sell something. The driver kept looking forward as the boy continued to bang on the window. The young boy looked over his shoulder, signaling to someone nearby. All of a sudden, another boy who appeared to be around the same age began banging on the passenger side window. They were sticking their arms into the car through the windows like vultures, trying to grab anything they could get their hands on. Then a third boy came.

The boys successfully pushed the windows down, shoving their hands inside the car and grabbing the driver's GPS. There was a white truck in front of us, a black car behind us, and no way to escape. The driver remained calm given the circumstances.

"*Vámanos! Vámanos! Vámanos!* Go! Go! Go!" I yelled at the driver, but there was nowhere for us to go.

The driver fidgeted around, trying to lock the doors, but he couldn't figure out how. Then one of the boys on the passenger side opened the door and threw himself in the car. By that point, the driver had started moving forward. He continued driving as the boy's body hung halfway out of the door, albeit at no more than five miles per hour. Finally, the boy jumped out of the car and started running behind it with his friends. Eventually, we got on the highway and lost them.

I'm pretty sure the driver was in shock. I know I was. If the boys had been successful, they would have walked away with my external hard drives, a MacBook Air that I had forgotten to back up, all of my filming equipment, and my Guinness receipts and proof. Luckily, as a smart traveler, I always made sure to keep my external hard drives and passport in my money belt under my shirt and pants. My credit cards, phone, cash, and license were stuffed in my sports bra.

For the remaining twenty minutes of the drive, the car remained silent, with both the driver and me on high alert. The traffic was relentless, and I could tell the driver was on edge, worried that if he was forced to stop, the same thing would happen all over again. I was nervous too.

I later learned there's a name for incidents like this: red-light robberies. After that experience, I educated myself about which countries posed the greatest threat for red-light robberies. To this day, I always feel nervous at red lights at night and keep a careful eye out.

YEMEN

Rather than taking a private charter to Socotra Island in Yemen, Guinness regulations required that I take public transport. This particular trip involved taking a public bus from Oman to Yemen, a far riskier way to travel than the tour agency or private charter that most travelers and tourists take. Instead, I had to risk entering the mainland in a way that is completely foreign to Western travelers.

In times of political uprisings or terrorism, the US government requires its citizens to leave Yemen. If that need were to arise during my visit, without access to a tour agency or private charter, I would be left to my own devices. This is not necessarily a situation anyone wants to be in, for sure.

I chose to spend the hours between sunrise and sunset in Yemen. Locals cautioned me not to push my luck with an overnight stay as an American woman traveling alone. My time there was particularly risky because, at the time I was due to arrive, President Donald Trump had been in office for twenty-eight days. Already, he had suspended foreign nationals from the Middle Eastern countries Iraq, Syria, Iran, Sudan, Libya, Somalia, and Yemen from entering the United States. Understandably, both the citizens and governments from these affected countries were appalled at Trump's decision. I was too.

I feared that because of Trump, I would be unable to complete my expedition. Many of the banned countries, including Iran and Iraq, backlashed, forbidding US citizens to enter their country. By a stroke of luck, I had already visited Iran and Iraq in the winter of 2016, so I was in the clear by the time the ban was put in place in

January 2017. Fortunately for me, Yemen didn't instate a ban, and I was able to both enter and leave the country without incident.

Normally, I don't care much for politics, but I started to care about it a lot during Expedition 196. My education about the election came from global media rather than the American press. It was clear to me that anyone but Trump should have won from an international perspective. But, of course, this isn't how it played out.

TUNISIA

In the still of the night and early morning hours of December 1, 2015, I wandered the streets of Sicily, searching for a Wi-Fi connection. I wanted to let my parents know I wouldn't be able to communicate with them for the next several hours. I was about to embark on a fourteen-hour journey to Tunis, Tunisia by ferry.

Tunisia was the first Islamic country I visited that had recently experienced a massive and devastating terrorist attack. On June 26, 2015, the deadliest nonstate attack in the history of modern Tunisia occurred with the Sousse shootings. Thirty-eight people, thirty of whom were British, were massacred in the course of enjoying a day at the beach on vacation. Less than six months later, I made my way to the port of Tunis alone.

The journey felt strange. The ferry was filled primarily with men who were making the trip to stock up on goods for their families in Tunisia. I was one of the only women in line for the ferry and was bombarded with questions from male guards and questioned about why I was entering Tunisia alone as a woman.

Since I didn't have much of a budget, I wasn't able to afford a cabin. Instead, I slept on pieces of cardboard, surrounded by Tunisian men. Despite the fact that I tried to find the most quiet and secure place possible on the ship, each time I moved, I was followed by men wanting to sleep near me. It's safe to say I didn't get a moment of sleep for the entire fourteen hours I was on that ferry.

I felt vulnerable floating out there in the middle of the ocean, one of the only women on a ship full of Muslim men. The one thing that offered me solace was that, as I had learned on one of my first solo trips to Egypt at the age of twenty-one, Muslim men are not allowed to touch foreign women. If a Muslim man does touch a foreign woman, he is subject to arrest. I was told this straight from the mouth of a policeman in Egypt. Whether or not this is true in all Muslim countries, I don't know. But it was in Egypt, so I just kept that thought in mind whenever I traveled to countries with a large Muslim population.

When our ferry finally docked, I turned on my GPS only

to find that alas, there was no signal. My phone didn't pick up a signal, either. I knew my parents had to be on edge waiting to hear from me, thanks to the constant threats of potential terrorist attacks in the wake of the Sousse shootings.

The stress and fear I experienced on the ferry were left behind once I set foot in Tunisia. In fact, it ended up being a life-changing experience. Despite all the unfortunate media attention, I found both the land and people of Tunisia to be both intriguing and peaceful. My eyes were opened to a history, kindness, and culture unlike any other I'd experienced. Even today, Tunisia remains one of my top ten favorite places in the world.

Tunisia is a great example of pushing through my fear; taking the calculated, necessary risk; and discovering a faraway land that's a hidden gem.

Tunis, Tunisia

Tunis, Tunisia

CHAPTER 5

THE PRICE OF SOLO TRAVEL

We are all alone, born alone, die alone, and—in spite of true romance magazines—we shall all someday look back on our lives and see that, in spite of our company, we were alone the whole way. I do not say lonely—at least, not all the time—but essentially, and finally, alone. This is what makes your self-respect so important, and I don't see how you can respect yourself if you must look in the hearts and minds of others for your happiness.

—HUNTER S. THOMPSON

I think we've all reached the point where we no longer have the energy or desire to keep moving forward. Those moments where, no matter how much you've tried or how immense a quantity of time and energy you've devoted to a single purpose, you feel you have nothing left to give. All you want to do is give up and let go.

It can be incredibly tempting to do exactly this when you're pushing through these times alone and there's no one else to drive you forward. Particularly as a solo traveler, I experienced the desire to give up several times throughout my expedition. In the end, I pushed through. I'm so glad I did.

PAPUA NEW GUINEA

Many people are afraid to travel alone because they fear falling ill with no one around to take care of them. For some reason, that thought never crossed my mind. Maybe because I realized that some form of 911 exists nearly everywhere, and in my experience, random strangers are often willing to help. However, an experience during my travels in Papua New Guinea made me realize how nice it would be to have a companion along to re-ice my head towel or fetch me a glass of water from the sink.

While in Papua New Guinea, I found myself feeling utterly depleted and helpless. This was a particularly difficult experience for someone who hates accepting help. However, after spending five days straight with the blinds closed, unable to so much as leave my bed, I finally succumbed to checking myself into a hospital. I knew I had to find out what was going on.

Not only was this the only time I got sick during the expedition, but it was also the most painful and debilitating illness I'd ever experienced in my life. From the moment I arrived in Port Moresby from the Solomon Islands, I felt sick. I'd had no more than four migraines throughout the course of my life up to that point, but it was still enough to know that the migraine I was experiencing in Papua New Guinea was different.

I spent five days in bed with peppermint tea bags placed over my eyes and a cold ice cloth over my head. My body ached, my sinuses were blocked, and my headache was so intense that even breathing felt like a challenge. I had no one to call to help me except AIG, which promptly found a local hospital within safe proximity to where I was staying. This was important because, at the time, Port Moresby was plagued by gangs, break-ins, and gunshots, even in broad daylight. The city is still considered among the most dangerous in the world. The hotel staff wouldn't let me walk outside alone and called me a taxi to take me to the hospital.

Once I arrived at the hospital waiting room, I sat down on one of the plastic blue stacking chairs covered in dust and brown stains. I was so depleted, I did not care. The room was cramped and filled with at least two dozen other patients.

My worst fear was that I had contracted malaria. I had

just come from a multiday stay in the Solomon Islands, where I failed to take antimalaria medication. Although naturopaths and doctors would not agree with my choice, I was grateful I had at least covered myself in 100 percent DEET, which I always carried with me. If you have never tried DEET, it burns and numbs your skin. Good luck if it gets anywhere close to your eyes or mouth. But hey! At least it fends off the mosquitoes that carry malaria and dengue.

Along with other malaria strains, Papua New Guinea is known for housing the *worst* strain, *falciparum* malaria. This strain is the only one that causes cerebral malaria, which affects the brain and often leads to a coma or death. I had three mosquito bites, and as a hypochondriac, I was sure one of them was malaria. At that point, I felt like I was dying and wasn't sure how much worse it could get.

The nurse drew my blood in a small, square room with light-blue walls and florescent lighting. Even the hospital wasn't an escape from the mosquitos, which were flying all around the room.

Later that day, I called in to get my results. My white blood cell count was dangerously low, but my results came back negative for malaria. Like so many other aspects of Expedition 196 that continue to remain a mystery despite the fact that I lived through them, I still don't know what mysterious illness took me down in Papua New Guinea. What I do know is that I've never again been as sick as I was there.

NEPAL

Of all the places and circumstances through which I've traveled, including deadly winding roads at 10,000 feet, I've never experienced altitude sickness like I did in Kathmandu, Nepal. With an altitude of 4,500 feet, to me (and to most people who have lived in high altitudes), that doesn't sound like much. Lake Arrowhead, where I lived prior to the expedition, has a higher altitude than Kathmandu. Never once did I experience any problems there. But, for some reason, every waking moment I spent in the intriguing city of Kathmandu was plagued with headaches, nausea, and a strange wheezing sensation in my lungs. I didn't have asthma, so this was baffling to me.

Not to mention the fact that it was monsoon season. On a massive deadline to get some additional visas stamped in my passport, I very much wished I'd had a partner along who could just do it for me, leaving me to lay in bed and sleep off the sickness. Instead, I found myself trekking through streets flooded with two feet of water in a fight to beat the clock and send my passport back to the visa company so I could grab a few more visas. I made it to FedEx just in time to send off my passport.

FRANCE

Throughout the expedition, I developed an uncanny habit of missing terrorist attacks by less than seven days. I traveled to Dhaka, Bangladesh, on July 6, 2016, just five days after the July 1 mass hostage shooting of twenty-nine people in that very city. The shooters were targeting non-Muslims like me.

In France, my margin of error was even slimmer. I arrived in Nice, France on November 14, 2015, just one day after the ISIS attack that took the lives of 137 people.

I was on a tight schedule as I made my way to give a keynote session to a university in Copenhagen. En route, I was traveling through Italy, France, Luxembourg, Belgium, and the Netherlands. On the train from Monaco to Nice, there was an eerie, sad feeling in the air. I exchanged glances with a girl sitting across the aisle from me a few times. It was clear we were on the same page. She looked empty and sad.

When we arrived at the first stop in France, it was clear the country was on high alert. Their borders were closed. In France, "closed borders" means that you in fact *can* enter but that border officials and security are checking passports. I watched quietly as the French police came on board to check passports, look passengers in the eye, and remove any person or luggage that looked suspicious.

When my turn came, they looked me over, but didn't ask for my passport. Since I already had it out, I handed it to them anyway. The officer looked at it quickly, smiled, and moved on.

Meanwhile, the two young, tanned men sitting across from me had a very different experience. At a glance, my best guess is they were from Northern Africa or the Middle East. I remembered noticing these two guys when we initially got on the train and thinking, "Those are exactly the type of guys border control is looking for, just based on their appearance." As I had assumed, the police escorted them and a couple of other young men off the train. It felt racist to me, although, since the police were on high alert the day after the attacks, I guess I didn't blame them.

I arrived in France to find it permeated by a weird feeling that I'm guessing usually isn't there. It felt like a mixture of uncertainty, sadness, and curiosity. Although, at the same time, this description is just an approximation because it's not really something I can explain. I wasn't afraid to be in France, but I was disheartened by what had occurred.

It was a cold and cloudy day, and Paris felt like anything but the City of Love. All the restaurants were empty, and the streets were barren. I was just about the only person who seemed to be willing to "risk" sitting outside to enjoy a Nutella croissant and espresso. This was my first time in Paris and my first chance to experience all of those things everyone raves about when they talk about this wonderful city.

I decided to take a walk toward the Eiffel Tower. As I stared at the lit-up structure, I noticed a young woman who was also alone and staring in silence. We struck up a conversation about what had happened the day before and how disheartening it was. The woman's name was Pernilla, and she was traveling from Sweden. She told me she had been eagerly awaiting her trip to Paris. Due to the attack, Pernilla's friends bowed out of the trip, but she marched on, refusing to let the terrorists ruin her long-anticipated vacation. Of course, it was a different sort of vacation now, but realizing she had the courage to face reality head on left Pernilla feeling like a strong and enlightened solo female traveler.

Undeterred, the two of us enjoyed a steaming cup of coffee together at a French café, and we still keep in touch to this day.

Paris, France

CHAPTER 6

COMPOUND LIVING

If you're going to try, go all the way. Otherwise, don't even start. This could mean losing girlfriends, wives, relatives, and maybe even your mind. It could mean not eating for three or four days. It could mean freezing on a park bench. It could mean jail. It could mean derision. It could mean mockery—isolation. Isolation is the gift. All the others are a test of your endurance, of how much you really want to do it. And, you'll do it, despite rejection and the worst odds. And it will be better than anything else you can imagine. If you're going to try, go all the way. There is no other feeling like that. You will be alone with the gods, and the nights will flame with fire. You will ride life straight to perfect laughter. It's the only good fight there is.

—CHARLES BUKOWSKI

Ever wondered what it's like to live inside a compound? Me neither. However, certain experiences on Expedition 196 led me to find out. More than just a fenced-in and guarded living space, life on a compound is an experience that also involves tight transportation and major planning. In my case, though, there wasn't any time to plan, which led to some interesting experiences.

SOMALIA

The armored four-door taxi SUV I was being driven in charged through four steel and concrete gates that were lined with armed guards. Our SUV was both led and followed by white pickup trucks filled with men holding machine guns. I took it all in from my vantage point of the dark-purple-hued back-seat window.

Two men were in charge of escorting every hotel guest from the Aden Adde International Airport in Mogadishu to the hotel, regardless of their nationality or gender. They sat in front; I was in the back. One of these men, the hotel staff manager, swiveled around to face me. "Look, there's an explosion site," he said, pointing out the window. "It happened two weeks ago."

To my right, I saw what looked like a hole in the ground, marking the site where a bomb had destroyed another nearby hotel.

Upon arriving at the hotel safe and sound, I was greeted by Yosef, the on-site hotel manager.

"Welcome to the Peace Hotel!" he said. "Astur, please show Cassie and the other two guests to their rooms."

Astur, the concierge, nodded and took me and two other guests, a couple, to our separate rooms. On the way, Astur pointed toward a closed door.

"This is the 'safe room.' Please go into this room and close the door if you hear an explosion. The room is well stocked. We have to be prepared."

I opened the door to my hotel room and locked it behind me. It was a large, barren, dark room that overlooked the compound where I was staying. There were two windows, one of which opened to the roof of the building next to me. However, since an explosion at the Peace Hotel had occurred several months before, about a dozen men were currently hammering, drilling, and performing repairs up there.

Throughout my stay, I kept a careful lookout through the thin, see-through, eggshell-colored drapes. To be honest, I stayed in the same outfit for pretty much the entire time I was there, with the exception of draping a blue shawl that I purchased from a local woman selling them within the compound over my head and body.

I'm not the kind of traveler who sits in her room, reluctant to explore new terrain for fear of a potential explosion. So back into the armed vehicle the guards and I went. Once again, both pickup trucks followed in front and behind. Gate number one to the compound lifted, then gate number two, then three, then four, until we were out in the open and vulnerable.

The hotel staff remained on the radio constantly to make sure that the extremist group, Al-Shabaab, was not in the immediate vicinity. When the coast was clear, the guys gave the go-ahead to disembark the vehicle and head to the fish market.

The skies were gray, the air was gray, and the grounds were a light clay color. We walked briskly toward the fish market as men yelled, "Sister! Sister!" I came to learn that men call women "sister" in Somalia; it's kind of like a nice way of saying hello. Smells of rancid fish filled the air as we entered the market.

I began to take pictures with my DSLR, but only once I was told I could by officials. I took some pretty vile pictures of fish innards and blood. Like most fish markets in developing countries, flies filled the air and lived on the fish. There were blood and guts spilled everywhere, an obvious safety hazard, but the fish was still considered edible in some places like this.

We then ventured over to the beach, where we saw fishermen actually catching the fish. As we stood there, one of the guards got a radio call that Al-Shabab was in the neighborhood and we had to move out quickly. He pointed toward the west, and said, "They're over there. Too close." As we drove back to the compound, he pointed out more explosion sites.

At least I got a little bit of beach time, a happy moment in Mogadishu.

Mogadishu, Somalia

Long before I reached Somalia, I had come to accept my potential death. Though I wanted to finish Expedition 196 before it happened, I often wondered what everyone would think if I did meet my end in the course of the journey. Based on the degradation and endless constructive and not-so-constructive criticism I received on social media, I assume people would have thought that I was a naive, privileged white girl who didn't know which end was up.

The online hate and false accusations I received from not only strangers, but also from fellow travelers alike, was shattering. I could never accept that the people in countries like Somalia and Afghanistan were so kind, yet the online world was a force to be reckoned with—a *negative* force to be reckoned with. The online sphere made me hate human beings, including myself. But the real world made me grateful for the people whose paths I crossed. What a juxtaposition.

AFGHANISTAN

I was on edge from the moment I woke up at 3:00 a.m. to get ready for my flight to Kabul, Afghanistan, because the hotel I had planned to stay at cancelled my reservations the morning I was due to arrive. They explained it would be unsafe for me to stay. To my knowledge at the time, this hotel was the safest option, so I found myself in a massive conundrum.

At the very last minute, I booked another hotel. This hotel had experienced a suicide attack from the Taliban just a year before, which killed nine people. People who were just enjoying their breakfast and working out in the gym when, suddenly, they found themselves victims at the hands of the Taliban.

For some reason, prior to the morning of my departure, I wasn't too nervous to travel to Kabul itself. Maybe it's because Emirates flies there from Dubai, so it somehow felt safer since Emirates is one of the safest and most luxurious airlines in the world. The compound I chose at the last minute did make me a tad concerned, though. I wrapped my hijab around my head and disembarked the plane. Aside from the lack of air-conditioning and long lines, my entry went smoothly. But boy, was I gawked at by local men—more so than any other Middle Eastern or Muslim country I'd ever visited up to that point.

As had been the case in Somalia, here, too, entry into the hotel required that we pass through multiple gates before gaining access to the compound. Gate number one, red and steel, slowly opened. The taxi I was in parked while the hotel guards used a long stick with a mirror at the end to examine the underbelly of the car for explosives. We drove through another gate, where we had to exit the car while dogs sniffed around, and our luggage was examined. While this was happening, I was told to sit in a six-by-three-foot room, where another small woman was waiting for me. She examined me to make sure I was all clear as well. Cameras recorded me as I placed my bag through a security scanner much like you would at an airport, common procedure in war-torn countries. I then walked into the next room, where they checked my luggage as I stood by. Finally, they pushed open the heavy steel doors, which gave way to the beautiful, clean, and colorful hotel lobby.

Check-in was smooth, and the concierge asked if I wanted a tour of Kabul. I agreed. After all, I hadn't come all this way just to sit in my hotel room and be left to wonder what Kabul was actually like, right? I threw on my hijab once again and headed out the door.

We grabbed a taxi to an area in town that was relatively safe and full of cool things to see, like markets. Many women wore full burqas that covered their entire face. Green and black barricades caught my attention at every corner. I snuck a few photos, but one of the guards caught me and told me to delete it, so I did. I wasn't allowed to speak to fellow women, let alone film them, even if they agreed. Their husbands were the decision makers, and anyway, women were forbidden to be on film.

Sadly, the Kabul river was filthy, and the streets were covered in garbage. Men sold live chickens and women sold beaded necklaces on side street carts. I filmed a vlog and collected video footage for the documentary, interviewing a little boy and a man along the way. I was quickly informed by my translator and guide that the man I interviewed was uneducated and, therefore, lacked an understanding of American people, politics, and foreign women.

"Muslim men are not allowed to interact with Muslim women unless they are their wives," my guide said. "However, Muslim men are allowed to shake hands with or say hello to foreign, non-Muslim women if they so choose."

When I reached out my hand to introduce myself, the man I was interviewing reluctantly looked at my guide, then looked down at his black leather jacket and shimmied the sleeve over his hand for me to shake, which I did. Based on his stern facial expression, he didn't seem to like Americans, despite the fact that he had a perfectly friendly one standing right in front of him. He looked back at his two buddies, who were a bit more chipper to see me than he was, and he chuckled with them whenever I asked a question and my guide translated.

All in all, I could have stayed out much longer, but I felt that half a day exploring Kabul was all I could handle at the time. I was intrigued not so much by city culture, but by the small village culture of Afghanistan. Specifically, the villages in the mountains, where I hear there's some pretty good skiing.

I could tell I was in for a long wait when I walked up to the line for border control at the airport on my way back out of Kabul. I must have spent an hour and a half standing in that line. Not surprisingly, I was the only Westerner— let alone woman traveling solo—in that line. The man standing behind me struck up a conversation. He was six feet tall and wore a brown *thawb*. He was from Kabul but spoke perfect English. He told me he did a lot of business in Dubai. We talked about peace and what our individual definitions of it were, which ended up being pretty similar. He honestly seemed like a nice, good-hearted person.

After we had been talking for about ten minutes, he said, "Do you see those three men standing in line wearing all white?" He looked back at them, smiled, and waved. They waved back. "Those are my friends," he continued. "They're in the Taliban."

For a split second, I couldn't believe what I was hearing. First of all, I wasn't in the least bit surprised that it was true. What *did* surprise me was he'd openly admitted such a thing to an American.

I instantly replied, "You're just telling me this because I'm an American and you think I'll be scared."

"Well, are you?" he asked.

Truthfully, I wasn't scared in the least bit. In a strange way, it was actually kind of exciting to be among the men who have destroyed so many helpless lives. It was like I was in a real-life movie, in a situation from which few walk out alive.

"Are they going to blow up the plane?" I asked.

"Nah, they're just normal guys," he replied. "They have to make a living for their families like any other person out there. They don't like to kill, but it's the only thing they can do to support their families. They travel for work, but these guys rarely cause harm. It's only during organized events."

Suddenly, I understood and felt all the more close and united with these men who are feared by so many. They were humans too. And the man behind me had a point: we all need to make a living to survive. After all, the whole purpose of my expedition was to make a living for myself once I successfully finished. One thing that many Westerners, and especially Americans, don't understand is that sometimes these jobs involve death, risk, destruction, and nonsense. When there is no other option, how are these men to support their families? I guess you have to look at both sides, no matter how disturbing and unrelatable one side might seem.

As we passed through security, I let the three men go in front of me. I noticed they did not have to put their luggage through the security belt or step through the metal detector. They were given the go-ahead by security to just pass on through. Meanwhile, my bag was searched, and I was interrogated. For a few minutes, I didn't think I'd make it on to the Emirates flight, but once I did, I noticed the three men sitting in the first two rows, alongside the man who had been behind me in line.

The man in the brown *thawb* waved hello and gave me a smile as I passed by him to get to my seat toward the end of the plane. Adjacent to me was a family: a mother, father, and two girls. I struck up a conversation with the younger girl, who knew English despite the fact that the rest of her family knew none. We chatted for the entire flight. It turned out she was accepted into a private school in the United States, which required her family to move from their home in Afghanistan to a newer and safer living environment in the United States. Tears of joy trickled down her face as she explained how excited she was to leave their destructive environment and start anew. We bonded, and I was so thrilled for she and her family.

Kabul, Afghanistan

Kabul, Afghanistan

CHAPTER 7

FEMALE EXCEPTIONS AND EXPECTATIONS

USA, COSTA RICA, ITALY, AND BURKINA FASO

Of all the evils for which man has made himself responsible, none is so degrading, so shocking or so brutal as his abuse of the better half of humanity; the female sex.

—MAHATMA GANDHI

Since I'd never experienced any form of abuse from a man in my life, I felt invincible when it came to traveling solo. I could never understand my female friends who were afraid to do things alone, even though, like me, they had never experienced any abuse.

The world was my oyster, and I knew that if a man ever tried to touch me without my consent, I would kill him. I have always been a strong female. In high school, I secretly wanted my senior project to involve me becoming a competitive body builder, but I settled on facilitating a Global Warming Awareness Day instead.

I always practiced "what if" scenarios in my head just in case, but even my hypothetical anger for men who would attempt rape or abuse was so strong that my confidence overrode any potential irrational fear. I felt free and unstoppable.

USA

One day in-between my first round of world travels at age twenty-two, I was working a double shift as a concierge/valet/fire lighter/whatever-else-they-needed-me-to-be at a high-end hotel in a small New England town. It was located in the serene, rolling hills of Litchfield, Connecticut. I had always dreamed of staying in one of the hotel's intricately and uniquely designed cottages. Being an employee there was another matter. I felt enslaved by management, who consisted of a rough-around-the-edges woman and a disrespectful, rude, impolite, contemptible man. As a hardworking female, I expected to be treated fairly and with respect. This story gets worse, and I share it to make the point that it is important to maintain high standards for what you expect from bosses and employers. Learn from my experience and don't let a work situation get this extreme.

A major blizzard was beginning. In this rural area, blizzards mean you better get inside unless you have a pickup truck. As the skies darkened and the flurries fell harder, my boss demanded we kids continue to work our asses off until our shift came to an end. I made a miniscule mistake, the specifics of which I can't remember. I tried to discuss it with the boss, but he wouldn't listen to me. I slammed my fists on the counter and demanded he pay attention to what I was saying.

"You're fired!" he yelled in response. "Go home immediately!"

By that point, the ground was covered in at least twelve inches of snow, and I did not have a car.

"How do you expect me to get home in this blizzard?" I asked. "Can't I just stay in one of the rooms or keep working until it calms down?"

"I don't care! Just get the fuck out of here," he yelled again.

By early that evening, the boss man had fired two of my coworkers, as well. His desire for power got the best of him, and because of it, he nearly cost us our lives as we scrambled to leave. I had no one to pick me up and no way of getting a ride home. There were no taxis, no busses, and no trains in these parts. Thankfully, I was wearing a pair of the Hunter green boots the hotel sometimes gave us to wear for our labor work, so I was able to walk through the snow. The cold was grueling, with temperatures in the teens. It was a windy whiteout. Had I been wearing the ballet flats I wore to work that day rather than the boots, I would have likely gotten frostbite in the course of my walk home.

I had already traveled a bit by this point but was itching to travel more. Maybe that contributed to my decision to hitchhike back home. Only, there were no cars out, and the trucks were few and far between. Finally, after I had walked about two miles, a pickup truck stopped. A nice man asked if I needed a ride. I sat in the passenger seat, fighting back tears.

When I finally arrived home, the storm had knocked out the power, which frequently happens in small towns during blizzards. My mom, dad, and I sat huddled under blankets as we ate some canned chili. It was at that moment I promised myself I was never going to work for a man again, and that I was going to do everything in my power to never suffer financially. To this day, I have never worked for a man.

When your days are planned around your income or lack thereof, money begins to consume every waking moment of your life. I always wanted to become wealthy, to be one of those prestigious bullet ants. I set a goal to make that happen by the age of thirty. As years passed, I realized that being a bullet ant doesn't necessarily translate to income, but rather, the positive impact a person is able to have on millions—if not billions—of people. It involves inspiring others to live their best lives and reach for the stars.

As I reflect on all this at twenty-eight years old, I can humbly say I've impacted a vast number of people based on the hundreds of thousands of positive messages I've received and the articles that have been written about my journey.

COSTA RICA

When I was eighteen, I studied abroad in Costa Rica and Nicaragua through Long Island University (LIU) Global College. Growing up, I knew in my bones that the world must be a positive and enchanting place, and the media and movies had to be fabricating stories about horrifying things like kidnappings, rape, and hostages. One thing is for sure, neither media nor movies have ever really painted a positive picture of solo female travel.

Walking down the street in Heredia, Costa Rica, I constantly heard human animal sounds, but it was often difficult to figure out exactly where they were coming from. Things like, "*Bambocciata!*" and "*Mwwwahhhh,*" followed by a high-pitched kissing sound. The sounds were faint enough and seemed to be coming from various locations—through the cracks of buildings, from rooftops, from behind me, or from someone driving by.

As this went on, I became increasingly angry. These male catcalls made me feel disgusting and degraded. I understood this was part of their culture, and that the Costa Rican woman responded to these calls, but as an American, I was appalled and frustrated.

From that point forward, the male gender began to seem disgusting to me and served as a source of anger. When you live through enough degrading experiences as a young woman, it becomes challenging to find the beauty in a gender that views women as sexual (and otherwise inadequate) objects. But at eighteen, this behavior was a revelation to me, and I was disappointed to learn that most men don't respect women, and they feel they can say whatever they please, even out in public.

One day, I volunteered at an art class at an elementary school in rural Costa Rica. Even the little boys who were no more than six years old asked me out and made sexual remarks behind my back. They also made the same smoochy sounds as the grown men in Heredia did. To me, this showed that, no matter what age, all men showed the same disrespect towards women.

During orientation in our first week in Costa Rica, the university made us all (men included) aware of the need to be cautious and watchful while traveling alone. We were told to be mindful about our alcohol intake and to hide our belongings when we were out in public. And for that matter, all of the time. They handed us all pepper spray in case of emergency. (That pepper spray, by the way, has lasted me to this very day.)

One night, I went out to dinner with some of my fellow students. Afterward, my friend and I grabbed a taxi back to our host families. It was about 10:00 p.m., and we had both had a couple of Imperials, Costa Rica's most favored beer. Despite this, we were still sharp. We knew we had to be since we were out and about at that time of night.

The taxi drove about twenty minutes to drop me off. I got out of the cab and waited at the wrought iron gate for my host brother to let me in. From the darkness, I watched as the taxi backed up and drove away with my friend inside. I didn't think much of it at the time.

When I went to class the next morning, everyone seemed a bit somber. I walked up to my friend, who was surrounded by a few classmates. They appeared to be comforting her.

"What's going on?" I asked.

That's when I learned that, after dropping me off, the taxi driver drove in the opposite direction of my friend's host family's house. He stopped in front of a green house, which she believed to be his. He proceeded to use the child's lock feature, locking my friend inside the car, and began to touch her. She said had she not threatened him with her pepper spray, he would have raped her.

My friend's experience stuck with me for life—but even still, I felt invincible.

ITALY

Between the years of 2010 and 2012, I traveled alone to roughly twenty-five countries. Of these countries, I lived in nine of them. This was my time to explore; to be a poor, nomadic backpacker; and to do whatever it took in order to keep traveling. Of course, this meant I took odd jobs working in hostels, where I swept floors, changed bloody and bed bug-ridden sheets (which led me to get bed bugs myself on three occasions), and ate scraps from the kitchen.

I was to work at a bed and breakfast in Umbria, Italy, in exchange for free room and board. Umbria borders Tuscany, so you can imagine how alluring it sounded to spend a few months of that autumn exploring the region.

It took me days of hitchhiking to get to Umbria. By the time

I got there, I was burnt out from traveling and just wanted to hang my hat for a few months. The man who owned the inn was in his mid-fifties at the time. Little did I know I was his only volunteer. Since it was low season, it ended up being just he and I tending the inn. I'd been in this situation before, working under a male employer abroad in exchange for free room and board. For some strange reason, I was never hired by women who owned inns. Just men.

This man made me eat lunch and dinner with him and limited my ability to explore, even though he provided me with a bicycle, which I utilized to flee into the hills whenever possible.

Since it was low season, there weren't really any guests around. One night, after I'd been working there for a month or so, I fell asleep reading the one book I brought with me, *Walden and Other Writings* by Henry David Thoreau. At the time, it was only the second book I had ever read cover to cover (Jon Krakauer's *Into the Wild* was the first). Hours passed, and I fell into a deep sleep. At 3:00 a.m., I was awoken by a heavy, repetitive knock on my door, accompanied by a male calling my name. "Cassssiieeee, *Casssiieeeee.*"

I knew it was the owner, but I was scared. Why was he knocking at my door in the middle of the night? I stayed silent.

In his thickly accented English, he said, "If you don't open de door, I will call de police!"

I threw my clothes on, quickly packed my backpack, and opened the door, determined to leave.

"Why are you packed?" he asked. "Come make love with me."

"Are you kidding?!" I responded. "What the fuck are you doing? You're old!" When you're a twenty-year-old-woman, a man in his fifties *does* seem old. After all, he was my parents' age.

Angry that I refused and called him old, the hotel owner took my backpack and threw it down the stairs. Then he pushed *me* down the stairs. I scrambled for my phone in an attempt to Skype my parents, tell them what had happened, and ask what I should do.

Before I could make the call, the owner said, "Get out! I'm calling the police! If you hang around my hotel and use the Wi-Fi, I will have you in jail for working illegally in Italy!"

Despite his threats, I managed to quickly call my parents. They were frantic. I had no options that night. I had to get out of there any way possible, so I sped off, running as fast as I could. Then I hid in the bushes when I heard a car coming.

Looking back, I now understand I had nothing to be afraid of. After all, I was not receiving pay. But knowing how I had been treated by male authorities in the past, I decided to hide. The owner did, in fact, call the police. I watched from a bush as he yelled at them to find me. The police drove around for a while but didn't spot me. When I saw that the coast was clear, I began the six-mile walk back to Perugia in the darkness. I turned on my cell phone's flashlight and held it to my back so that passers-by could see me.

It is thanks to these early experiences as a solo female traveler that I felt, with knowledge and a little luck, Expedition 196 would be a breeze for me.

BURKINA FASO

One twenty-four-hour flight and short taxi ride later, I arrived in Ouagadougou, Burkina Faso. Burkina Faso is known as one of the safer countries in Western Africa, but just a few months prior to my visit in 2016, there was an attack on a hotel. Al-Qaeda and Al-Mourabitoun took more than 140 people hostage, killing thirty of them.

AIG Travel made me aware of the potential dangers of Burkina Faso in advance. In situations like these, I always budgeted a small stash of cash to put toward staying in secure hotels, as opposed to winging it, as I would typically do. I was advised to stay at the Sopatel Silmande Hotel.

After a swift check-in, I proceeded up to my room and swiped my key card. Burnt out from my long haul, I threw on my underwear, chucked aside my eyeglasses, and fell into bed. Since I only carried a small, carry-on backpack, my clothing consisted of seven pairs of underwear, two sports bras, two pairs of socks, one black tank top with a built-in sports bra, one long-sleeved black shirt, one black down jacket, two pairs of black leggings, one pair of baggy gypsy pants and a black scarf. I wore all black, so no one could see the dirt on my clothes. I only washed my clothes when I stayed somewhere for longer than three days so I could hang them to dry. Usually, this happened about once a week.

The rest of my pack was filled with my DSLR, tripod, lighting equipment, external hard drives and batteries, portable projector, business cards and peace bracelets to hand out, a small toiletries bag, travel pillow, a pair of dressy flats for my meetings, the one pair of running shoes that touched down in every country (sponsor me!), and an emergency bag filled with a flashlight and first aid kit. There was no room for a pajama set, so I always slept in my underwear. Hey, a trip like this is about making sacrifices!

I was in a deep slumber when, at 2:00 a.m., I awoke to the blurred vision of my door slowly opening, and a crack of light becoming wider. I can't see much without my glasses, but I could make out a tall figure slowly walking into my room and closing the door behind him. In a panic, nearly naked and sightless, I fumbled for my glasses and began to shout, "Who is that? Get out! Get out now!"

They speak French in Burkina Faso. Unfortunately, my knowledge of French was none. I did not know how to say "get out" in French. But, despite the language barrier, the intruder seemed to understand the sentiment. He became frantic and quickly left.

"How could he have gotten a swipe key to access my room?" I wondered. Ultimately, I came to the conclusion that he must have been an employee.

Here's why.

The next morning, I went downstairs to let the reception know what happened the night before. There I found four men and no women working. As I explained what happened, they looked down silently, as if they were ignoring me.

When I'm being wronged, I become very angry. I have never tolerated being taken advantage of. I smashed my fists on the marble counter and demanded that they check their security footage and look into what happened. I've found that smashing my fists on the table always at least elicits a response as opposed to being ignored. I had booked two nights but refused to stay for the second night. Since I was out of my room before 10:00 a.m. (and given the circumstances), I requested a refund for the second night. I was determined not to stop until they gave it to me.

If I had let every hotel or hostel take advantage of me like this in the course of the 196 countries I visited, I wouldn't have been able to finish my expedition. Instead, I would have been penniless. I was on a tight budget. Letting go and moving on from a situation like this one and losing $150 in the process was not an option for me, so I had to at least try in every situation like this that occurred to get my money back when applicable.

The men at reception ended up calling the police to take me away. The police were, of course, all men. They did not speak English. I had no other choice at that moment but to walk out of the hotel $150 short. The hotel would not call me a cab, nor would they allow me to wait for a cab if I called one. In that moment, I realized I was being taken advantage of because I was a woman. In this situation, I had no say. I was surrounded by men who knew they were in the wrong. This incident was a wake-up call, and the first time in my life that I realized I was not invincible.

A kind man from France who was also staying at the hotel called me a cab and let me know I was not in the wrong. He told me he'd seen the male hotel staff act the same way to other women staying there for a convention. I'm not the only one.

THE MEN I MET ALONG THE WAY

I don't want it to sound like I have a problem with men. But for the sake of female readers who are curious about my experiences with males as I traveled the world, I want to be fair and honest. There are many men who have traveled the world, and several who have traveled to every country. In fact, the record I broke was originally set by a man. By attempting to become the first woman on record to travel to every country, my goal was to prove that women can achieve the things that people believe only men can do.

But there's a dark side to achieving in a world dictated by men, and the world of travel isn't any different. Over and over throughout Expedition 196, I saw degrading and negative blogs, posts, and articles written about me. At first, I could not believe what I was reading—completely biased remarks and fabricated information about my travels. Then I saw those remarks were being written by men—men who also travel.

Halfway through the expedition, when the media began following my travels and the public began to catch on, I attracted just about every male blogger out there who had great intentions of tearing me down in order to strip my records and accomplishments. Some of these men had large social media platforms, though not nearly as large as what I had accumulated by that time. I felt reluctant to speak up, knowing their online tribes would take the writers at their word, and suddenly, I would have a massive crowd against me.

I left it alone, but I was angry. I had to learn that these men were envious of a woman in the same industry as them and of greater caliber. The gnarly side of travel that most people don't see is the envy that exists among both men and women within the industry. Sadly, it makes the business of travel less enjoyable and more toxic. This was not the first time I witnessed male envy directed at women who achieve at higher levels. It's an unfortunate reality of the world we live in.

One traveler and blogger took the time to understand me. He could very much relate to what I'd done and how deeply the online hate affected me. He went on to become a friend and almost mentor-like figure until the end of my expedition. He gave me hope in mankind and softened my outlook on the gender as a whole.

With all of that said, there were also many men throughout my trip who took the time to help me or teach me something new about their culture or life in general. In places like Mauritius and the Maldives, I was welcomed and taken care of by male hosts. And in places like Libya and Somalia, my life depended on the hospitality and kindness of men.

Erbil, Iraq

THE WOMEN I MET ALONG THE WAY

A female who travels alone has both advantages and disadvantages. While I've experienced my share of unfair and sexist situations, I've also found myself at an advantage most of the time.

Border control officials in many countries flirted with me, and if I smiled back, they'd stamp my passport and let me through with ease. I feared if I did not smile, they would be reluctant to let me into their country, even though I had all the proper documentation and visas to enter. A smile on a girl can get her a long way, but I'm not the type of woman who will do so just to enter a country. Often, border control gave me a hard time because I clearly did not care in the least about engaging with them. I owe that man behind the glass nothing, but I do owe the country itself a positive outlook. I bonded with women I met on the expedition over our shared experience of being at a physical disadvantage when it came to men.

In Iran, I was taken under the wing of a lovely couple, Rezvan and Mehdi. The wife, Rezvan, took me around Kish Island, which included a brief visit to an all-women's beach. Cell phones and cameras had to be left at the front, and all women who entered had to place their belongings through a security belt and be groped by a female guard. I could not believe it when I walked on the beach to find several women basking in the sun completely naked. In Iran of all places!

It was shocking that women could be so free in a country that is restricted to the point where a Muslim woman is subject to arrest for not wearing her hijab. It was wonderful to see that females had a place to be free and feel safe, away from men. I told Rezvan that I wished a beach like this existed in the United States.

The positivity and happiness of women, even despite their

limitations, really shone through in countries where you'd never expect it. In Libya, for example, I was welcomed into the home of a local family, where the mother loved making her children and children's guests (including me) delicious and wholesome meals. Even though she had an assistant chef, she spent all day in the kitchen, creating incredible meals like *usban*, a spaghetti soup that consists of sausages and tomato sauce.

In North Korea, my twenty-four-year-old guide, Miss Lee, was such a happy young woman. She was thrilled that, despite the political circumstances, she could show me around the country she so loved.

In Bolivia, I was seated at the very back of a run-down bus on my way to Chile. It was a long, eight-hour journey, and of course, halfway through, the bus got a flat tire. We were stuck in the heat for another hour.

Bus rides are my favorite place to reflect and observe, and to listen to podcasts and music. But on this particular bus ride, I was seated next to an indigenous Bolivian woman dressed in ragged clothes who didn't speak a lick of English. Her hair was dark brown and woven into one, long braid. She was missing every other tooth. She was heavyset and carried with her two large sashes. One of her bags was filled with carrots and corn, and the other, endless green oranges and coca leaves. (Coca leaf is the raw material used to make cocaine, and the leaf is popular to chew on at high altitudes as it combats altitude sickness.)

This woman must have eaten four handfuls of coca leaves and three oranges an hour throughout our eight-hour ride. I was a rookie and could barely eat two of the oranges she generously offered me. Despite the fact that I only speak basic conversational Spanish, I was able to understand quite a bit of what she told me about thatched roofs, mountainous terrain, and the local traditions of Bolivia. She was the first friend I met on the expedition.

Atacama Desert, Chile (traveling with a woman from Bolivia)

And then there was Hadeel from Syria. Before she hopped in the taxi, she hugged her two friends tightly and said goodbye. As we drove away, I noticed her eyes well with tears. Hadeel and I really connected, and it turned out those two young women were her sisters. This might be the last time she would see them for years.

Originally from the Western side of Aleppo, Hadeel and her husband went to Latakia for vacation. Upon their return, they found their entire home had been completely destroyed by rebels. Her husband was able to gain acceptance as a refugee in Germany, braving the Aegean Sea from Turkey to Greece, and then trekking along the Balkan route for twenty-five days before reaching Germany. Hadeel had to wait a year and a half before she was granted access to live with him in Germany.

At just twenty-five, she lost her mother; at twenty-seven, her father. When I met her, Hadeel was twenty-eight years old, nearly the same age as I was. Here she was, facing yet another journey that would test her—taking her first flight, completely alone, and leaving her country for the first time in her life in order to be with her husband in Germany.

I couldn't have felt more humbled to have met Hadeel and to hear her story. But more importantly, I was grateful for the opportunity to tell her that everything was going to be okay, that she was strong and would make it through.

Latakia, Syria

We all have a story that is being written from the day we are born. Only we truly know that story from the inside out. We're all pained in some way and by something, and no two experiences are ever the same. We're all so incredibly different in so many ways, yet we are also much the same. The connection I had with Hadeel was so special. At the same moment in time, we were both venturing out into the unknown, out of our comfort zones. Both of us were a bit scared, sad, and excited, all at once.

Whether it's connecting over beaches, food, cooking, or a long journey into the unknown, I was able to experience true depth with so many amazing women throughout Expedition 196. These women chose to live their lives how they wanted to, despite everything they were told they couldn't do.

I have always looked up to Amelia Earhart and other female travelers before me as sources of inspiration. Sometimes, though, inspiration also lies within the people we meet at the most unexpected of times. In these people, we find both similarities and differences. There's no right or wrong way to travel, have an experience, or live this life. It's yours and yours alone. As my travels have taught me, even those in the most pressing and limiting situations can find ways to make life their own. Know that and use it to pursue the unimaginable. It might just mean inspiring the person sitting right beside you.

Al Ghaydah, Yemen

CHAPTER 8

DETAINED

GRENADA, UNITED ARAB EMIRATES, LIBYA, THE CONGO, AND NORTH KOREA

To the well-organized mind, death is but the next great adventure.

—J.K. ROWLING

The greatest fear of most travelers is being denied entry into a country they have traveled so far and spent so much of their money to get to. Growing up in the United States of America, where, according to the US Department of State, only 10 percent of Americans held passports back in 1994, I am often reminded of the fear many people have of traveling anywhere outside our country. (Note: This mindset is changing, as of 2018, where the number of passport-holding Americans has risen to 40 percent.)

The government and media instills the fear that certain countries are bad, when, in reality, they're actually great and are relatively safe places. What *is* bad, though, is getting caught in the wrong place at the wrong time and finding yourself in one of those theatrical moments that you only hear about on *60 Minutes* or *Unsolved Mysteries*.

In my early backpacking days when I couch surfed my way around the world, my friend often shared with me her thoughts on the dangers I was subjecting myself to in traveling this way. However, once she saw my continued couch surfing adventures around the world on social media, she decided to try it herself domestically. In the end, she became an ambassador, hosting couch surfing events throughout the East Coast of the United States.

The same was true for another former good friend of mine. We lifeguarded together when I was in college, and I told her of my plans to travel the world. She was resistant to the idea, and she told me about the many ways in which the world was a dangerous place. Her thoughts and beliefs were based on the media, as she had never really traveled much herself. She went on to work a nine-to-five consumer sales job and lived with her longtime boyfriend throughout her twenties. By then, the travel bug had bit my friend, but her boyfriend held her back, and she was scared to go alone. When I told her about Expedition 196, she suddenly gained the confidence to quit her job and travel solo. I'm told she is now an advocate for solo female travel.

These scenarios and so many more demonstrated to me the importance of proving people, especially women, wrong about their misguided notions of the dangers of traveling. I consider it my calling to show through example that the world is generally a positive and relatively safe place, just waiting to be explored.

KAYLA'S STORY

Having said that, of course the world is not entirely free of danger. Five months before my departure for Expedition 196, a twenty-six-year-old American woman named Kayla Jean Mueller was working with Doctors Without Borders in Syria when she was held captive and killed by ISIS. I learned of this as a twenty-five-year-old woman about to travel into Syria myself. Similarly to Kayla, I was visiting as a humanitarian who represented nonprofit organizations, promoting peace and responsible tourism.

I was really taken by Kayla's story. Sometimes things just don't seem real until they happen to someone of a similar background to your own, who is doing something similar to what you are about to do. Before, I had always assumed if something like that were to happen to me, at least my home country would pay up and get me out. But Kayla's story made me face up to the fact that my home country does not pay ransom. If you are captured, you're shit out of luck.

The risk Kayla took is one that many men and women take on a daily basis in order to fight for their country and provide aid and education to those who need it most in other countries. And I was about to do the same. I was about to take a risk with the understanding that I could potentially face captivity and death by one of the world's most feared terrorist groups at the time, ISIS.

While I made sure to take all the necessary precautions, at the end of the day, it was a risk. I was mentally and physically prepared for any potential situations that might lead to my demise. Kayla and I both entered Syria within the same relative time frame, but only one of us came out alive. When a person enters a foreign country, they are automatically and legally under the power of that country. That country has the power to do with them what they please, no matter what rules or regulations exist in the traveler's country of origin.

Despite Kayla's experience, the thought of being detained still wasn't much more than a nebulous thought for me. Until I was actually detained. It was only then that stark reality and fear hit me like a thousand bricks.

GRENADA

I decided to travel to Europe and Latin America right off the bat at the beginning of Expedition 196 while the rest of my visas were still processing. I began in Trinidad and Tobago and worked my way up the Caribbean.

When I arrived in Grenada, things took a turn for the worse. I carried a large Ziploc bag filled with vitamins meant to last me for the entire leg of my journey. Carrying these vitamins in their original containers would have taken up too much space in my bag. Whenever I had to fly back to the States for visa and passport swaps, I'd also replenish my Ziploc. In it were women's multivitamin tablets, vitamin C tablets, valerian root, probiotics, and turmeric tablets.

It was a nice, sunny day in Grenada when I landed and cleared the border. I was waiting for a taxi to take me to my hotel-style bed and breakfast. I tried to stay in local hotels or B and B's whenever possible in order to support the local economies of the countries that I visited. I didn't feel the need to use my safety reserve funds for a hotel in Grenada because it's considered a generally safe and touristy country. An hour passed, and I was still waiting. I used my data to call the taxi company, which was expensive, but I needed to know when they would arrive.

By this point, a couple of men were circling around me like

vultures. One man in light-colored jeans and an orange American Eagle polo top called over to me. He was seated on a bench outside the departure area. I looked at him and then looked away. "Who is he?" I wondered. "And why won't he leave me alone?" I decided it was best to ignore him. This was always my tactic with men.

But then he came over to me and said, "Come with me."

"Who are you?" I asked.

"The police," he responded, showing me his badge.

Another man in an actual police uniform came over and escorted me inside. The men wouldn't say anything to me, and I started to feel increasingly vulnerable. In fact, I had never before known vulnerability like I did at that precise moment. They led me to a room with orange walls, a heavy brown table, and two half-broken black plastic chairs. They closed the door behind me. I politely asked them to either leave it open or invite a woman inside so I would feel safe. They brought a woman in who stood and said nothing for the entire time I was in the room.

I repeatedly asked what was going on and why they were going through my things. They refused to answer and started getting an attitude with me. If I feel I am being mistreated, I will speak up. It's always been my nature, and

I did not let this experience deter me. Since I was not in the wrong, I felt okay being a little tenacious with them. They thought I had smuggled cocaine into the country by placing it in the tablets I carried in my Ziploc bag. I rolled my eyes at that point and let them do their thing. Their thing involved two hours of testing each vitamin for cocaine with a little machine. When they were finished, they let me know they were embarrassed but that, two weeks prior, two young women from the US had smuggled cocaine into the country.

Being detained in Grenada was a major wake-up call for me. It was an experience I needed to have. I had to come to terms with the fact that I wasn't invincible. Just like anyone else, I, too, could be detained or captured. But you know what they say: the first time is always the scariest. You are unable to leave or ask questions, and you can't use Wi-Fi or call anyone. You're literally at their mercy and the guards dictate your next moves.

Little did I know then, though, that this was only the *first* time. As it happened, I would go on to experience border trouble in some of the world's toughest countries.

UNITED ARAB EMIRATES

I learned a lot in the course of the 255 economy plane flights I took over the course of the expedition. I knew to be the first person off the plane—or to at least be at the front of the line once we disembarked. Sometimes this meant sprinting. It was worth it, though, because the last thing I wanted to do when I arrived in a country was wait in line for an hour at border control, as most people do.

As usual, I made it to the front of the line at DXB (airport code for Dubai, United Arab Emirates, Dubai International Airport), where there were two rows open. Despite the fact that the line to my left began to quickly pile up, for some reason the border control officer didn't call me up. Instead, he said, "Go to the back of the line. We're not open."

Instead of going to the back of the line next to me, I stepped over the foot-tall red stanchion, placing myself behind a short line at the front of it. Was my reaction selfish? Sure. But after all the sprinting, I figured I had earned my spot at the front of the line. Not to mention the fact that I had a flight to catch and I was about to miss it. Apparently, the people behind me saw my predicament, and graciously allowed me to scoot into the front of their line.

The border control officials were not feeling so gracious. Again, they ordered me to the back of the line. My anger erupted in the face of a situation that was completely and utterly unfair to any logical human being. I went to the back of the line, forcefully threw my backpack on the ground, left it there, and paced around to blow off some steam. I had been awake for sixty-two hours straight by that point. Expedition 196 was almost complete. The end was in sight, and all I wanted to do was to make it to the finish line as quickly as possible.

One of the security officers took me into a nearby private room, as any logical security officer would do in this situation. I didn't blame him. "Please," I said, "let's just save ourselves some time. Put me in jail right now."

I was completely depleted. It felt like the inside of me had been torn to shreds. The combination of the continuous stream of hate mail, failed visas, dangerously low numbers in my bank account, and lack of accomplishment despite the thousands upon thousands of hours I'd put into the expedition had left me with no hope for humanity or my career. I was spent, and at that moment, being thrown in a jail felt like nothing more than a good distraction from my stress and responsibilities.

The officer looked at me and made a gun motion with his hand. He pointed it to the center of my head, and said, "If I were a security officer in the United States, I would shoot you right now."

"If I had a gun right now, I would shoot myself," I thought.

"But I'm Muslim," he continued, "so I won't. Do you want to travel into Dubai?"

"Not really," I replied. "I just want to get to my next destination."

"*Do you want to travel to Dubai?*" he asked again, this time with more emphasis.

"Sure," I said. "I've already been ten times before, but for the sake of you wanting me to say 'yes,' my answer is 'sure.' But I really don't care to at this very moment."

With that, the officer walked out of the room.

Looking back, I was acting out like a child, and the border officials were in the right. But it is human nature, and almost unavoidable, to allow one's emotions to take over when in the throes of sleep deprivation. I first learned this lesson during *Naked and Afraid*: adults turn into children when they're not sleeping properly. When a person goes for more than twenty-four hours without sleep, their brain begins to turn on them in ways they normally couldn't even imagine. I wouldn't expect anyone who has not tested these limits of exhaustion to understand.

Border control didn't allow me to pass through to the

airport. To this very day, I might still not be welcome in the UAE. It's a shame because it is a great country.

But at least I managed to catch my flight.

Dubai, United Arab Emirates

LIBYA

At the time I traveled to Libya, the country was experiencing a lot of instability, with kidnappings occurring in broad daylight. I arrived late at night, around 11:00 p.m. Border control was confused about why I was traveling alone and wearing all black with a tripod sticking out of my gray backpack.

US citizens traveling to Libya are only allowed a business visa, which I had obtained in advance. Customs didn't want to let me in, but this situation didn't scare or even bother me much. My tour guide who greeted me upon arrival was surprised and doing his best to talk them into letting me in.

But he wasn't exactly successful, and two hours later, the Libyan officials had decided I was in the CIA because of my black clothing and tripod. Despite this, they joked with me as I sat in their small waiting room. They were very kind and understanding people. After much deliberation, I was let through, though I'm not exactly sure what made them change their minds.

I was happy to be in a place that I had waited so long to visit. I was sad to see the power was out in many of the buildings in Tripoli due to the rebel forces and Islamist armed groups that had controlled central Tripoli for the past two years. Nonetheless, I loved Libya and its people, and can't wait until I can visit and see more of what the country has to offer. If it were up to me (and not Guinness, with their transport and time regulations), I would have ventured to the desert by camel to soak in the immense allure that Libya has to offer.

Instead, I met with the minister of tourism, Mr. Almabrouk Muhamed Ali Attargi, and provided him with my IIPT Credo of the Peaceful Traveler. This credo was a simple document created by the International Institute of Peace through Tourism that outlines the values and principles between travelers and their hosts. He was a really kind person.

Tripoli, Libya

DEMOCRATIC REPUBLIC OF THE CONGO

A little south, in the also politically unstable and land-locked country of the Democratic Republic of the Congo, I experienced my first and only bout of bribery.

Let me start by saying that the DR Congo is naturally very captivating. However, it's also very impoverished, and even the airport authorities are itching for a dime. Upon my arrival at the health check point in the airport, two women demanded my yellow-fever card. I gave it to them. I only got the card back again because a nice older woman who also worked at the airport bribed them to return it to me. This little guardian angel told me to staple the card into my passport next time.

When it was time to depart DR Congo, I found myself face-to-face with the same two women. They were very recognizable with their blonde and purple hair, and thinly penciled eyebrows. Again, they asked me for my yellow fever card. After scrolling through it quickly, they informed me I was missing my polio vaccination, which they said, "was required in order to *depart* the country."

"Come in the back with us, and we'll give you the shot," they said.

Take my word for it, Goma Airport is just about the last place in the world where anyone would want to receive a random "polio" shot. The polio vaccine was not a requirement in any country in the world, let alone Africa (however, there are at least a half-dozen countries where it is recommended for stays over four weeks).

I knew they were toying with me. "Do you want $100?" I asked. "I'm not going in the back to get a shot." They both looked at each other, and then turned to me. "Thirty dollars," one of them responded.

I handed over my "exit fee" and then proceeded to the gate.

NORTH KOREA

Let's be honest: this is the part of the chapter you've been waiting to read, right? Ironically, my hold up in North Korea wasn't as exciting as many of the others, but still, finding yourself held at North Korean customs under any circumstances makes for a pretty shocking situation.

Traveling to North Korea was like walking on a thousand eggshells for three days straight. For me, it was an enjoyable experience, aside from the rain. I was there in August of 2016, when the American University of Virginia student, Otto Frederick Warmbier, was being held in a North Korean jail. Sadly, we all know how that story ended: ten months later, he was dead under mysterious circumstances.

As I was departing Pyongyang International Airport, I

stood at the immaculately clean border control, sheepishly looking down at shiny floors as the female agent examined my visa and passport. My tour guide Miss Lee and the Chinese tour guide stood on the other side of the railing, whispering to one another and glancing over at me, then at border control, then back to me again.

"No, no," the agent said.

Uh oh. Something was wrong. I watched a look of surprise and shock pass over the tour guides' faces.

"What's wrong?" I asked kindly. Of all the horrific scenarios I'd visualized myself in over the years, North Korean prison was the last fear I wanted to realize.

I waited another five minutes, as confusion set in. By ten minutes later, a bead of sweat trickled down my face. Fifteen minutes later, I heard a voice over the loudspeaker: "Last call for the Air Koryo flight to Beijing." Thirty minutes later, and my nervous system felt fried.

Finally, the agent came back, stamped my visa (which I couldn't keep, but I did take a picture of), and let me catch my plane, which I almost missed.

I later learned that, apparently, the tour guides had failed to provide a departure form that was required to leave

North Korea. At the time, I had assumed the issue was the coffee cup that I forgot to put back in the breakfast room or the picture I took in the subway station that didn't include Kim Jong-un and Kim Il-sung's entire bodies.

Pyongyang, North Korea

August 24, 2016

Things started out pretty rough today. I checked out of the hotel in Shenyang at 6:00 a.m. to make it to my flight to North Korea. I was pretty bummed out because I was exhausted to the point of delusion. Before checking into the flight, I had to put all of my things in a storage locker, including my camera and cell phone.

I went to the international terminal at Shenyang Taoxian International Airport, where I thought they'd have lockers. But when I arrived, it was pretty much just a room where people could leave their suitcases. They did have a few lockers, but none with keys. I was super nervous about this. They told me there were cameras in case someone tried to steal anything. But for me, this wasn't enough. Then I started getting really nervous because time was getting tight before my flight, which departed from the domestic terminal. I decided to check in first, then come back to figure out the storage situation.

It took about fifteen minutes to get to the departure terminal. I had woken up with a massive headache thanks to a nasty combination of skipping my morning coffee and dehydration. When I went to check in, the guy said I didn't have a ticket number. I got nervous. "Fuck, not again," I thought. Chase Bank had a bad habit of blocking my card or shutting it down for "fraud" when I least expected it.

I waited on hold with Chase for quite a while, only to learn that the ticket itself was never issued because they assumed someone had fraudulently used my card. I went to the ticket counter and was told it was too late to buy a ticket for the flight I'd intended to take to Beijing to catch my flight to the Democratic People's Republic of Korea (DPRK). To be specific, I was about five minutes too late. I literally broke down. If I couldn't get to North Korea, it would represent a wasted week of travel, more money, and another night at the hotel, which would amount to half the money I had designated for North Korea.

I ended up buying a ticket for the 10:40 a.m. flight. It was supposed to arrive at 12:10 p.m., which meant I would be cutting it close to the time when I was designated to meet up with my travel group. I decided it was worth a shot anyway.

I grabbed some coffee and water, then ventured off to tackle the storage situation again, this time in my departure terminal. The scenario was the same, but at least the airport staff made me feel more comfortable.

The flight from Beijing to Pyongyang was weird. It felt similar to going to Iran, Afghanistan, and Somalia. I was on Air Koryo, North Korea's only airline and the only way to get in and out of the country. It was a reasonably sized plane and about half full. I took up my own row, per usual. The flight attendants were so interesting. They looked like they were all cut from the same cloth: each of them looked the same, with the same hair, same makeup, same stance, and same smiles, all at the same time. Each attendant wore a pin with a picture of Kim Jong-un's face and another man, who I think is his dad.

Literally, every person on the plane who was North Korean was also wearing that pin. They were all so very proud. North Korean music was playing when we got on the plane, and then we watched NK TV, which probably plays on repeat on every flight. They served us these perfect looking "burgers" in a plastic container that were actually pretty good. They also served a disgusting purple juice, no water.

As I watched the flight attendants throughout the flight, I began to feel that they were like dolls. They seemed enslaved but, strangely enough, also happy. I spoke with one of them on the way back to China, and she was the sweetest thing. It sounded like she loved her country. She went on and on about how fresh the water tasted, how clean and crisp. My impression is that North Koreans are not the enslaved, painfully depressed, and starved people that we hear about. Not from what I saw, at least. They're brainwashed by Kim Jong-un, sure, but they're happy.

I was kind of nervous when we arrived, but then I saw how harmless border control looked. Way less intimidating than the Senegal border control, which was atrocious. I walked through border control with one of the male Chinese tourists and an adventurous Chinese girl, who were both about the same age as me. He was going to be traveling across the States soon. She worked in Angola, so we talked about the devastating brutality of certain parts of Africa for a while. She brought some really delicious Chinese fruits that we ate before she had to throw them out at the border control gate.

The guys at border control were really nice. On my declaration form,

I wrote down literally everything I could think of that was in my bag. Still, I forgot to document my USB and cords. They asked me if I had any books. I said no, but when the guard started signaling to my bag, I worried that maybe I *did* have books that I had forgotten about and would be punished or something as a result.

"Not that I know of," I corrected myself before realizing the officer was signaling the USB I had forgotten to list. Still, it ended up being okay. He asked my tour guide, Miss Lee, a few questions that I didn't understand, but neither of them seemed concerned. We were off!

The two Chinese travelers, Miss Lee, a Chinese tour guide, and myself, loaded onto a pretty decent bus, along with some other Chinese tourists. None of them spoke English, except for one who looked like Paul McCartney as a *youngin*. I was the only foreigner among about ten Chinese tourists. It was difficult, but Miss Lee made it better.

I honestly had no desire to see any of the city and all the fake crap everyone always talks about, but wow! Are they into Kim Jong-un. He. Is. Everywhere.

We got to the hotel. I was told it was the same place where the American student, Otto, had allegedly taken something and ended up being held for fifteen years' hard labor as a result. It made me nervous. I looked around for cameras. We went up to the room, which was moist and kind of shitty. Gross bathroom. Just a few towels. But there was a strange boom-box-style bedside table that looked like it came from the 1950s. It didn't play music yet had speakers. I wondered if this was their way of spying on us in the room. I decided not to say anything bad, even while vlogging, in case my accusations were correct.

Dinner was disgusting. We had Chinese food rather than local North Korean fare, which we were all disappointed about.

August 25, 2016

I had to share my room with another woman, since I didn't pay the extra $80 for my own room. She was a fifty-year-old Chinese woman who didn't speak any English but was nice enough. I couldn't believe how crude she was, though. I was in the bathroom, and she barged in and started pissing in the toilet. She burped the whole time, snored, got up in the middle of the night and turned on all the lights on multiple occasions. As a light sleeper, I didn't catch a wink.

We drove around all day, learning all about Kim Jong-un. There were so many Chinese tourists, it was unbelievable. I didn't see any Westerners.

We went to some friendship tower, which they only take Chinese tourists (and not Westerners) to for some reason. I'm not sure if it was one of those fake setups. Again, Kim Jong-un and the man I think is his father were everywhere.

Before lunch, I felt like ultimate shit—super nauseous and like I was going to shit myself. It's either malaria, Ebola, or food poisoning from dinner last night. We had lunch at a restaurant where they served us these little platters with really delicious food, including sweet mochi balls. After lunch, I was feeling a little better, but not much.

The highlight of my day was shitting myself on the side of the road in the pouring rain with sticks poking my ass. Apparently, this is the Chinese way to do it. Miss Lee said that if I were with Westerners, the bus stop would have involved an actual toilet. But since everyone else was Chinese, we just went on the side of the road.

We went to the DPRK–South Korea border, where guards showed us around. One of them was very tall and handsome. He looked at me a lot. Clearly, he knew I was a Westerner (the only one among one hundred tourists at the time), but he probably didn't know where I was from. He came over and started talking to me. Miss Lee translated. Basically, he said North Korea is ready to launch a massive missile nuclear attack on the US if we lift a finger at them. Blah blah blah. I've been hearing about this since I was a kid, but it's twenty years later and, still, no attack. All talk, no walk. Even if they did, we're all dying anyway, so what does it even matter? The world is overpopulated, so these sort of things—war, natural disasters, and disease—are earth's way of wiping out people in mass numbers to make room for more. It sounds shitty, but that's the way it is.

But back to the guard. I reached out to shake his hand and he squeezed my hand hard to show his power—probably as hard as he could without actually breaking my hand. It literally made me tear up. I don't know if I got a little emotional, because I was so excited to be breaking barriers by way of an American peacemaker and

North Korean soldier shaking hands, or if it was because I was afraid they'd hold me in North Korea per his request or something. Either way, it was powerful.

If the guard really hated Americans that much, he would have killed me on the spot or requested to hold me there. But he didn't. Instead, he kept looking at me and smiling.

After the border, we went to visit a native house where Kim Jong-un was apparently born, although it's probably not true. I stayed in the bus when we arrived because it was pouring. The bus was parked beside a massive water park, probably the park that was built for tourists that everyone talks about.

Next up was the metro, where I was kind of freaking out. Apparently, it's the deepest subway system in the world. It felt like we kept going down for ages, and I'm claustrophobic. At least it was really clean with a super nice decor. I was looking for the requisite photo of Kim Jong-un, and at first, couldn't find it. Then I looked straight ahead and voilà! There he was in all his gluttonous and prickly glory. He's a terrible person, so I don't feel bad for saying that.

We drove for two hours, and I was able to get some sleep on the bus, thank God. We then went to a restaurant where they seated us at a spinning table that served all sorts of North Korean food. The Chinese tourists ate their entire meal within about ten minutes' time, which is different than the slower pace I'm used to. There was also a lot of loud singing and dancing, which was nice for a bit but became very bothersome after a while. North Korean beer, I must say, is delicious.

Back in our room for the night, the woman who I was staying with called my name from the shower. I opened the door and she was in the bathtub naked, asking if I knew how to work the shower. I couldn't believe how open she was.

August 26, 2016

I'm back on the plane now, mulling over my thoughts and highlights from North Korea.

The people who praise Kim Jong-un remind me of the people who praise Trump. They seem so brainwashed. They're not unhappy. In fact, they actually seem quite happy with their lives and with him. They believe in him and everything he does.

The people of North Korea are impoverished, yes, but they're fed, they have houses, and, from what I saw, they're not homeless on the streets like many people in the States are. They aren't really suffering as badly as we think they are. Although, this doesn't apply to the people in the camps. I didn't see them and don't know what their situation is. Though I did ask, Miss Lee always diverted. I don't even know if free North Koreans know about the camps.

The North Koreans I spoke to were misinformed about a lot of things. My tour guide seemed oblivious to a lot of stuff. They know what they're told, what they see on their five TV channels that are chosen by Kim Jong-un, and what they read in their weekly newspaper, which is totally biased, but they don't hear what the rest of the world hears about them. I don't know if what I've heard is true.

It's strange, the things that stick, though. For example, one of the first questions Miss Lee asked me was, "So, how is Hannah Montana these days? I remember an American tourist showing me videos of her!"

"Oh, you know," I replied, "she's the same old Hannah Montana." It seemed like the best and easiest way to answer.

I don't know what to think about the staging that North Korea is known for. We drove around towns and through villages and saw how the locals lived, both the rich and the poor. Sure, we went to petty little monuments that were probably created just for tourists (like most other modern-day monuments), but I'm sure there's much more beauty if you venture out of Pyongyang and into the countryside. There's a whole other part of North Korea that no one sees (although they could if they wanted to). Tourists want to see the conspiracy and propaganda stuff, but I wasn't interested in that. If I were to go back, I'd go skiing, go to the mountains, and to the beach. It's nature that restores people's faith in countries that the media portrays as terrible and war torn. I'd love to see that side of North Korea, but I just didn't have the time.

In all honesty, I was super bored the entire time. Miss Lee kept talking about the United States, Americans, and war. I still don't understand why North Korea says they want peace, yet there are paintings and post cards all over the place of their military using machine guns and threatening the US. It seems so fucking extreme and unnecessary for them to project themselves in such a way. Almost embarrassing. They have so many paintings of guys with guns, and they're always talking about launching a nuclear attack, yet they've never been successful at it. It makes them look like wimps to me. Launch a nuclear weapon and get it over with or shut up. I think it's all a facade and seems like a bunch of BS. They want power like ISIS. Like Trump.

Pyongyang, North Korea

CHAPTER 9

LEAST EXPECTED

PAKISTAN, YEMEN, IRAQ, AND DOMINICA

We dream that we're all different. The reality is that we're all not.
—ANTHONY T. HINCKS

I found myself deep in thought as I stood at the back of an airplane. Ahead of me were two rows with three teal cushioned seats on each side. I placed my hand on the white plastic wall in an attempt to keep my balance as the plane cut through turbulent clouds.

"Please, miss, go back to your seat," the flight attendant said to me.

This moment would forever be engraved in my mind as the pivotal point at which all the curiosities I'd ever had about humankind were addressed.

I lost all sense of time as I realized each of those heads bobbing in front of me were made up of the exact same matter. Each head even went so far as to sway in the same direction as all the others. They all moved together in a cohesive, weightless, almost whimsical sway. "We're all just a head," I thought, continuing to observe.

Despite all the stories I've shared about the risk and hardship involved in Expedition 196, my ultimate mission was to promote positivity and safety in places where we might least expect it. We tend to cultivate and justify our opinions about other countries based on what the media—and, frankly, even books like this one—tell us.

But I want to share with you my experiences in six different countries. It was these countries that opened my eyes to the positive humanity and morality of our world. These are the same countries that are degraded the most in American and Western media; they're the ones that governments have made us fear for decades. The truth is that these countries are actually brimming with natural beauty, humanity, culture, kindness, and allure.

North Korea, Afghanistan, Somalia, Iraq, Pakistan, Yemen, Colombia, Sudan, and the Central African Republic. These countries are all regarded as among the most dangerous in the world. How about Tuvalu, Nauru, Kiribati, Djibouti,

Bhutan, Andorra, Brunei, Dominica, and Liechtenstein. Ever heard of those? I hadn't either.

I'm not writing this book to talk about countries that have a bad rep *and* where I might have had a bad experience. My goal is to be honest about the places that provided me a "least expected" kind of experience since that's one of the questions I seem to get asked the most. Also, I find great joy in experiencing the countries that people expect to be the most dangerous. I feel most at home in these countries.

I used to experience anxiety and panic attacks. Going to places like Syria and Somalia helped me let go of my anxiety. I realized, "You know what? That little bump on my finger that I worry is cancer—but in reality is nothing more than a bruise—would mean nothing if I was living in one of the world's most war-torn countries."

In addition to putting my own worries into stark perspective, visiting these places also helped me appreciate—and even find comfort in—the unknown. It made me comprehend things about my own priorities that I wasn't even aware of. Like coming to the understanding that I would rather take risks in situations where I might die rather than lying in a hospital bed from a debilitating disease that was out of my control.

PAKISTAN

One of my favorite countries was Pakistan, or "land of the pure" as it translates in the language of Urdu. Since the May 2, 2011 death of Al Qaeda leader Osama bin Laden (which, unfortunately occurred in Pakistan), the country has received an undeserved bad rap.

I will be the first to tell you that politics is not my strong suit, nor even of particular interest to me. So, without getting too deeply into it, what I will say is that it is so unfortunate that politics has deterred tourism from flourishing in a country that so rightfully deserves it. Pakistan is filled with culture and breathtaking natural beauty, from the Karachi beaches to the cloud forests of Lahore to the vast mountains of the Karakoram mountain range in the north.

I'm not trying to sell you on the place, but I do want to reiterate how safe I felt traveling alone there as a woman. Pakistan is unlike any other country I've been to. It's nothing like India, but it does have some culinary similarities. It is also very different from the neighboring Middle Eastern region, although certain similarities also exist.

In most Muslim countries, I showed my respect by covering my head in a hijab; however, in Pakistan, this wasn't required. They wanted me to be myself. After speaking to students in Karachi, Lahore, and Islamabad, I was so honored to plant the Pakistan national tree, the Himalayan Cedar, with dignitaries, teachers, and proud nationals of Pakistan that it forever changed my view of religion's place among humanity. They said a prayer of peace, and we began the planting process.

It was humbling to be able to connect with individuals who represented the Islamic religion—in a country that is so highly disregarded by the United States—to join in a moment of peace and serenity. Trump would never tell the US that beauty and kindness actually do exist in the Middle East, even though I'm sure he knows they do.

Lahore, Pakistan

YEMEN

Though I was only in Yemen from sunrise until sunset, I still had the chance to immerse myself in the culture and local heritage of the small towns that lined the coast: families enjoying their beach picnics, sesame oil being made in a rundown garage, the best chai tea I'd ever tasted, which came from a little shack with no doors.

The harsh reality of the poverty and lack of clean drinking water was devastating. For the first time in my life, throughout all my travels across developing nations, I was aware of little children and adults alike begging for water rather than money. I handed out water bottles to them but couldn't help feeling it wasn't enough.

I left Yemen feeling somber yet lucky and blessed for the moments I had with the locals, including a family that invited me into their home for a traditional lunch. Their house was made of straw and stone and was fairly large, perched on a hill with the sea just a short drop below them. I ate from my hands on the floor with the men in an empty room with only a large Persian rug and some floor pillows to sit on. The windows were open, and a relaxing sea breeze floated through them as I gazed out at a full view of the Arabian Sea. I felt calm and comfortable, and watched as the men took frequent breaks to pray.

Al Ghaydah, Yemen

The women were in another room, eating separate from the men. I walked over to the kitchen, where dirt covered the tile floor and the windows were open and without screens. The mother, who essentially served as the queen of the household, sat on the floor enjoying her lunch as large black flies buzzed around her and the food. She offered me a cup of tea, clearly very happy to have me there. I happily accepted.

The entire family was so taken aback by my appearance and culture, the latter of which they could only imagine. I was like an alien to them, but to me, they might as well have been family. I was invited into the daughters' room, which was bright and airy. One girl sat on the floor, painting her face with makeup that was tossed into a large plastic purple makeup bin identical to the one I had as a teenage girl. They were filled with giggles and curiosity. The youngest girl, who looked to be no more than eight years old, ran around in a torn red dress and bare feet. She covered her mouth and giggled as she looked up at me with her big brown eyes.

The entire family was strikingly beautiful. The men had big green eyes and were also curious and giggly in my presence. The older men were a bit more serious but still eager to spark conversation. This was another one of those situations in which we communicated without words yet still understood one another.

It was a scorching hot day, but the family was happy and content to spend their time together. I snapped a picture that only the men were able to participate in. (As was the case in Afghanistan, the Muslim women in Yemen were also not allowed in photos.)

I would have loved to spend more time, but I understood what a technically dangerous position I was in as an American woman. My Oman friend told me that news of my presence would travel fast, and the extremist groups would soon catch wind.

Yemen opened my eyes to a devastating but profoundly humane world that one cannot even begin to understand unless they're immersed in it—even if only for a day.

Al Ghaydah, Yemen

IRAQ

When I landed in Erbil, I couldn't believe how clean and safe it was. I was in Kurdistan, a relatively safe, autonomous region located within the northern region of Iraq. The area is highly disputed, which has made for quite a bit of friction between those who feel strongly that Kurdistan is an independent country and those who feel it belongs to Iraq.

Kurdistan is to Iraq what Greenland is to Denmark. Technically, Kurdistan is its own country, with a certain degree of freedom to act independently. However, it is effectively a subdivision or dependent territory of an independent sovereign state, that being Iraq. For the record, I was only required to visit sovereign states (in other words, nations), which meant that visiting Erbil and receiving a stamp that read "Iraq" technically counted as visiting the sovereign nation of Iraq.

To put this in context, Somalialand is an autonomous region within Somalia, and a relatively peaceful country compared to Somalia itself. So instead of going to Mogadishu, I could have traveled to Somalialand, which would still technically be considered traveling to the sovereign nation of Somalia, even though the visa requirements are different. I share this because I think it sheds some light on the complexities and precision involved in properly achieving this particular Guinness World Record.

When I traveled to Somalia, I emailed Guinness to confirm that traveling to Somalialand was sufficient. I didn't hear back from them in time, so, to be sure, I risked my life and entered Mogadishu. Some might argue that traveling to Erbil (where a visa is not required as a US citizen) does not technically count as going to the mainland of Iraq (where the visa processes are very stringent). But either way, both regions are one and the same when it comes to visiting the actual sovereign nation of Iraq.

Now that that's out of the way, we can move on.

The taxi driver who picked me up at the airport was a young man with porcelain white skin, bright red hair, and blue eyes. Immediately, I knew I had arrived in Kurdistan. I'll admit, it was a little bit shocking when the driver spoke Sorani instead of English because he looked like he might have been born in Ireland. I have always been intrigued by the Kurdish culture and particularly taken aback by the alluring beauty of both the women and men that comprise the region. Like my taxi driver, many of them have red hair and blue eyes. Others are bestowed with a beautiful tan color, which is offset by striking green or blue eyes. They look unlike any other people I've ever seen on this planet.

When I arrived at my hotel, I was greeted by men (surprise, surprise!). Extremely kind and welcoming men. They knew when to keep to themselves and respect my privacy, as a woman traveling alone.

I felt 100 percent safe going out and exploring on my own, and I headed directly to the Citadel, where everything was happening. Sure, I got stares, but generally speaking, there was a sense of respect as I wandered the streets and historical ruins alone, snapping pictures along the way. The Citadel closed at sunset, and as I was making my way down, the police stopped me to let me know it was closed for the day (in English) in a totally chill and nonthreatening way. I was grateful for their respectful and calm manner, which was in stark contrast to most of the police officers I'd experienced around the world.

Teenage boys were in awe of both me and my camera, and many chuckled as they asked me to take their photos. It was the weekend, and families and children were all out having fun and enjoying themselves in Erbil. A man in a beautiful costume poured me some traditional Iraqi iced tea. He was one of those nicely tanned men with green eyes. Kindness poured from his eyes. It was reassuring to know how safe Erbil really was, despite the fact that, just an hour and a half drive west, that wasn't the case.

I felt really happy in Iraq, and specifically in Erbil. It's a magical little place in the midst of chaos. When you get to know the people and heritage, it is truly captivating in all of the best ways.

Erbil, Iraq

DOMINICA

I have always been—and still am—terrified to fly over the water in small planes. But there was something about this particular flight that stripped away every ounce of strength and courage I was usually able to summon. On that particular day, dark clouds engulfed the usually bright and sunny skies of Dominica, giving way to a massive storm on the horizon. For the first time in my life, I did not want to leave a country.

During my time in Dominica, I experienced every variation of jubilation one can possibly experience. As we ventured higher over the mountains, we looked up at the sky and saw double rainbows encased in airy clouds peeking in from the overhang of the jungle rainforest. I got carsick on my way to Secret Bay, a beautifully sustainable luxury hotel perched on the cliffs of Dominica's northwestern-facing part of the island. But it was worth it. The hotel management took great pride in organizing an on-property tree planting to offset the carbon footprint necessary for me to get there. The dewy air made the hummingbirds flitting about seem even more beautiful and made the sunset seem even softer.

Dominica is one of those countries that has suffered terribly at the hands of natural disasters. It's a shame because of its natural beauty—jungles, waterfalls, beaches, gorges, and boiling lakes. I would be grateful to have the opportunity to visit again, but I'm afraid that, again, I would find it too hard to leave.

Portsmouth, Dominica

CHAPTER 10

EUPHORIA

MONGOLIA, ANTARCTICA, AND BHUTAN

All that I ask out of life is that it be constant and unending euphoria.

—ROMAN PAYNE

As I journeyed around the world on more than 255 flights throughout the duration of Expedition 196 (which, by the way, I will have completely offset by 2020), I spent most of my time being 99 percent sure that whatever plane I was on at the moment was going to crash. The cure? Jack Daniels duty-free whiskey, before and during most flights. I would even go so far as to drink secretly on flights to countries where alcohol was forbidden. I risked my freedom in Muslim countries so that, if I did die in a crash, at least I'd be drunk for it. Talk about a not-so-alpha female.

When each flight landed, I was shocked I had made it through alive. In those moments, I didn't want to die. Dying in a plane crash terrified me more than anything else— more than being captured by ISIS, more than being raped or kidnapped, and even more than going to jail in North Korea. Dying in a plane crash was my greatest fear, and the thing that made every other "normal" fear seem petty.

MONGOLIA

The common fears most people have usually made for an enjoyable experience for me. In June 2016, I was about to turn twenty-seven. I've always viewed birthdays as the one day of the year to reflect on living to see another day and to plan out how to live until the next. I believe everyone should take their birthday off of work and spend the day reflecting on their life. I've never worked on my birthday, even though it cost me at times. I always plan to take the day off of work months in advance. This is your life, and birthdays mark the day you opened your eyes for the very first time. You don't know how much longer you will have your eyes open, so observing this day is important.

For my twenty-seventh birthday, I secured a five-day sponsored stay in a remote yurt camp in Mongolia so I could reflect. I'd always dreamed of visiting Mongolia. I paused my Guinness Record attempt so I could take private transport deep into the wilderness.

The yurt camp had no cell phone reception, no Wi-Fi, no electricity, and no means of communication with the outside world. For five days, I was completely engulfed in my own existence, thoughts, and simple way of life. I had been receiving quite a bit of online hate that particular week, so I was thrilled that I didn't have to look at social media for five days straight. I have always had a hard time slowing down, but this trip really forced me to do so. I had the time and concentration to examine a blade of grass in all its glory and to take deep breaths of the crisp, twilight air under the stars.

One of the kindest and best friends I met throughout the course of my expedition was a canine named Jack. Jack was a wild Siberian Husky who followed me around everywhere, including inside my yurt. I had grown up with a Siberian Husky, so I was comforted by his presence.

To combat evening and early morning temperatures that hovered around thirty degrees, the yurts were powered by wood-burning stoves and a ton of blankets. The shower water, which was filtered from the river, was heated in an iron bowl that sat on top of a wood-burning stove. The hot water was then scooped with a large wooden spoon and ladled into an iron container that trickled bits of hot water. The toilet was located thirty feet away from the camp and built around a freshly made wooden enclosure that boasted breathtaking views of purple iris-covered fields, rolling hills of pine trees, and green grass.

I rode through pine-covered mountains on wild Mongolian horses that bucked with every horsefly bite. It was a bit scary, but Bataar, the local horseman, ensured my safety. Bataar was a rustic farmer who lived in a small, circular yurt with his wife and three young children. I visited them one day, and the kids could not have been more joyful as they ran through the fields and milked the cows, snot rolling down to their chin all the while. I, too, milked a brown cow under Bataar's direction. Only once before in my life had I ever milked a cow, back when I was homeschooled as a child. I'd forgotten how difficult it was.

Tuul River Valley

Later that week, I rode a yak down to the river for a calm raft ride with just me and two guides. They packed a steak-and-tomato sandwich that I enjoyed as I attempted to shoo the horseflies away. At any given time, roughly one hundred horseflies buzzed around the yak, which smelled like a mound of rotting carcass. The river was cold and still as we floated down it. When sunset came, I watched as the bulls grazed on the horizon, their silhouettes stark against the pink- and purple-hued sky. It was a perfect moment during this period of observation and self-reflection.

A complete lack of communication in the remote wilderness is one of those things that many modern-day civilians fear most. I actually thrived on it. With silence, you are faced with your flaws, your negative thoughts, and your inner demons telling you what could, should, or might have been. Allocating prolonged moments to be alone and uninterrupted with yourself and nature can sometimes make for the most healing experiences.

Tuul River Valley

ANTARCTICA

Speaking of remote, imagine a similar situation to the one I described in Mongolia. Only this time, instead of being able to drive three hours back to civilization, you're floating on a 250-person capacity boat in the middle of one of the world's most dangerous bodies of water. That was my experience in Antarctica.

On this particular day, I walked down the stairs to a delicious and plentiful breakfast buffet. I grabbed a few hardboiled eggs to take back to my small, round dining table. As I was sipping on my coffee, I watched in awe as both of my eggs flew off the table. At first, I couldn't tell whether it was me or the table that had tilted. I quickly realized the tables were mounted to the floor and that the entire ship was tilting to one side. I looked around and saw that everyone was walking at a forty-five-degree angle. It was one of the most interesting sights I had ever seen.

Over the loudspeaker, the captain announced that all passengers were to meet in the main auditorium. Whispers and curiosity filled the air as my fellow travelers and I wondered what was up.

"We have to cut our Antarctica trip short by a day to avoid the Beaufort category ten storm that is upon us," the captain said. "I'm very sorry, but we are about to enter the beginning of the storm, which could reach up to sixty-mile-per-hour winds and thirty-foot waves. Please prepare your cabins and secure your belongings. Take clothing hangers off the rack and be sure to take your sea sickness medication now."

That evening, we drank Argentinian Malbec and danced under the disco ball because when you are about to head into the worst of situations, it's natural human instinct to want to enjoy life as best you can. To us youngins, that meant swilling Argentinian wine and swapping fun stories.

We all felt the entire front of the ship lift, followed by silence for five seconds, and then the sound of a big *boom!* and a massive drop. This cycle continued again and again. Since it was dark outside, we couldn't actually see what was going on. The scenario I imagined was that the ship was riding massive waves, and when the wave crested, the bow took a nosedive. No matter where you were on the ship, it was hard not to focus on the whistling wind and the ship rocking from right to left and front and back.

The voice of our expedition leader Woody came over the loudspeaker. "Remember your cold-water immersion suit, which is located under your bed," he said. What could be more reassuring than being told you need a suit to keep you warm should you be thrown into the frigid Antarctic waters in the middle of the night?

I tried to pry open the steel porthole hatch that opened to a glass window in my room, only to find that the staff had locked it tight in preparation for the storm. I wanted to see the waves crashing upon my window as the boat rocked me to sleep.

Almirante Brown Antarctica Base, Antarctica

BHUTAN

I decided to pay the twenty-five dollars for a brief lounge stay, during which I could fill up on whiskey and coffee at Nepal's Tribhuvan International Airport. I had a bit of a journey ahead of me, and it was also the Fourth of July. I FaceTimed with my parents and said "cheers" to my fellow citizens back in America, as I was about to make my way to the most peaceful and least corrupt country in the world, Bhutan.

Once I landed at Paro Airport in the Kingdom of Bhutan, I realized that maybe the country is able to stay so peaceful because there are so few tourists. With a daily visa fee minimum of $250, many are deterred from visiting simply due to the high cost.

Bhutan is, in my opinion, one of the most underrated and euphoria-inducing countries in the world. At the time, only one airline flew into and out of Bhutan—Druk Air. Only a select number of pilots are allowed to fly into what is one of the world's most dangerous airports, Paro Airport. Pilots must be very skilled to navigate through 18,000-foot mountainous terrain and strong winds. Not only that, but the airport's dangerously close proximity to the surrounding mountains dictates that this navigation must be completed solely based on the pilot's judgment, without the help of any equipment. Not surprisingly, the flight has a reputation for being terrifying. Surprisingly, though, Druk Air has a pretty safe track record and not a single fatality to date.

Naturally, I had to drink before this flight, and that I did. I'm glad I did too. As the plane navigated through the Himalayan Mountains, thrusting to the right and dipping to the left, I felt weightless. This sensation was immediately followed by the feeling of a thousand bricks falling on my brain. I looked to my right, and it almost felt as if I could see into the living room of the house on the hill. We were *that* close. Until that moment, I didn't know a plane could drop and turn at a forty-five-degree angle simultaneously and still land safely.

Despite this horrific flight, Bhutan ended up being one of my top three favorite countries, in the company of Pakistan and, of course, America. From massive pink phalluses draped with serpents and twine that bring luck and rid homes of evil to free-growing and untouched marijuana to betel nut for dessert and, finally, to the majestic Tiger's Nest, Bhutan has got to be one of the most fascinating and captivating countries I've ever visited in my life. It was well worth the risk.

Paro, Bhutan

CHAPTER 11

TIME

CUBA

*Practice kindness all day to everybody and you
will realize you're already in heaven now.*

—JACK KEROUAC

This story deserves a chapter of its own because it's relatable to most people, and I learned many valuable lessons. This story brings tears to the eyes of all with whom I've shared it. It has to do with stereotypes. It has to do with the kindness of humanity. It has to do with how one moment in time can lift you up in the most dreary and hopeless of situations, and then restore your belief in the goodness of the human race. This single story shows clearly, and combines well, all the analyses I've made about the general state of our world and humanity as a whole.

If you've traveled—even to a distance no further than your

neighboring town—you know your view of that place was based on your own personal experience. You developed a sense of the people and culture in a way that no one else ever has before you. In a way that you likely can't completely convey to your family or friends. That experience is yours alone.

A single brief experience can shape your whole life. That's what happened to me more than 196 times. In fact, I have looked into the eyes of every people in every country of this world. From this, I understand the magnitude and bounty of this world and its people.

I've lived in the United States for twenty-eight years and have not been to the Statue of Liberty. I lived in Aguas Calientes in Peru for two months and only saw Machu Picchu and Cusco. However, in Jordan, a country I visited for three days, I met with the mayor of Amman; gave a keynote session to the students of Mashrek International School; traveled three hours to the Dead Sea and another three hours to Petra; experienced the bazaar, the archeological museum, and several other art sites; and experienced a mosque too. I slept a total of ten hours in those three days. A lot in a very short period of time.

Petra, Jordan

Dead Sea, Jordan

Here's the trick though. In order to capitalize on whatever little time you have to experience a place, it's essential to discard all stereotypes. Most countries have a specific, widely held, and oversimplified image of what it is all about. It can be very wrong. I made my greatest and most naive travel mistake in Cuba. I learned so much from it.

"How can you 'feel' a country you've only spent a short time in?" I hear this question a lot. All I needed was less than twelve hours to learn everything I needed to know about the people of Cuba.

I had just made the biggest mistake of my entire expedition and was completely helpless as a result. Crouched on the side of a desolate road in Veradero, Cuba, at midnight, I realized I would have to walk ten miles back to the airport.

Just twenty-four hours ago, I was departing JFK Airport in New York City, following a week at home securing visas and replenishing funds through sponsorship acquisition. Utterly wrapped up in my record attempt and future meetings, I, for the first time in the course of the expedition, failed to withdraw cash at the ATM before entering the next country.

At the time I visited, Americans were only allowed to travel to Cuba on a visa for "support for the Cuban people," which I selected at the JetBlue check-in counter. American banks and credit cards had been restricted in Cuba since the 1960s blockade. I knew this, but it had completely slipped my mind in the heat of the moment at the airport.

I arrived in Cuba at around 10:00 p.m. and hailed a taxi to the hotel. Halfway through the ride, my eyes opened wide when I realized I didn't have any bills on me. Naively, I figured the hotel would be able to assist me or that somehow, I'd get lucky and an ATM would accept my debit or credit cards.

The taxi driver dropped me off at the hotel. "Twelve pesos," he said. I ran in and asked the hotel if they could pay my driver, and then charge me the amount as an incidental fee upon checkout.

"Didn't you read the email?" the reception asked. "We cannot take US debit or credit cards—only cash. I'm sorry, but you're out of luck. You can't stay with us."

I looked to my right and saw what looked like US tourists happily walking about, enjoying their evening. I thought about walking up to them and asking if they could cover my stay and taxi in exchange for reimbursement and then some, via PayPal, but I quickly realized how sketchy that would sound. Why would they trust a young girl with a backpack?

The receptionist recommended I visit a Western Union to take out funds the next day. Since that day was Sunday and I was due to leave that night in order to make it to my student meeting in Mexico on Monday, it wouldn't do me any good.

I turned to the taxi driver and asked him to follow me to

all the ATMs in the area. At each ATM, I tried all four of my debit and credit cards. Not surprisingly, none of them worked. I walked ten minutes back to the hotel as the taxi driver drove beside me. I felt bad riding with him knowing I couldn't pay him.

Finally, I sat on the side of the road near the hotel and began to hyperventilate. An older couple from Spain came over and asked me what was wrong. The taxi driver explained to them what had happened, and they looked at me sympathetically. They didn't offer to help, and I didn't blame them.

In broken Spanish, I tried to communicate with and understand what the taxi driver was saying to me. It sounded something like this: *"Tiengo tres hijas, odiarfa que estuvieran en tu posicion, por favor, ver a quedarte con mi familia por la noche."* This translates to, "I have three daughters. I would hate for them to be in your position. Please, come stay with my family for the night. "

I looked up at him sheepishly and politely refused. But he continued to wait for me. He did not want me to be alone sitting on the side of the desolate street in the middle of the night. My plan was to walk the ten miles back to the airport and sleep there. The taxi driver, whose name I later found out was Diago, said his house was close by and he could drop me off there, where his wife would take care of me. He offered to take me back to the airport the next day so I could figure out what to do.

Diago worked all night long after dropping me off at his home, which was five minutes away. When I arrived, his wife and daughter greeted me with a smile. "I can't imagine what his wife thinks about her husband bringing home a young, blonde American girl at midnight," I thought. I felt embarrassed and intrusive.

His wife spoke a dialect of Spanish that I could barely understand. Under the florescent lights of their small, concrete house, she offered me a Pepsi and empanada and invited me to sit on the torn gray couch. There, we watched a Cuban game show on their 1950s-style television.

I couldn't remember the last time I'd felt so exhausted and numb yet also so immensely grateful. Diago's wife showed me to the purple toilet in case I needed to use it. She motioned that I would need to fill the bucket with water and then pour the water into the toilet bowl after I used it.

She then showed me to a room adjacent to the kitchen, where she had made up the bed for me. There was the bed with one small pillow, a white table fan, and curtains that were half tacked to cover the open window. She said goodnight with a smile and gave me a hug.

I have no idea how big their house was, but from what I saw, it consisted of no more than the living room, kitchen, bathroom, the room Diago's wife gave me, and one other room down a short hallway. The floor was covered with a light dusting of soot. As I tried to find a space on the awning to remove my contact lenses, I noticed all the nearly empty makeup and hair spray canisters. I turned off the lights.

When I woke up the next morning, I opened the door and looked down. Diago's wife was sleeping on the kitchen floor, atop a yellow one-inch-thick foam pad, with a floral sheet draped over her. It was at that precise moment I realized she had given me her own bed to sleep in. The other room was her daughter's.

Varadero, Cuba

She quickly got up and said, "Buenos dias, Cassie!" She proceeded to offer me a cup of Cuban coffee, which we drank as we waited for Diago to come back from his night shift to drop me off at the airport, where I'd wait for my flight.

Travel a little bit, and I guarantee you will find the kindness of humanity in even the most unexpected of situations. After living through several situations like this myself, I learned to ignore the things people told me about a country, good or bad. I left all preconceptions at the door in order to formulate my own opinions about each country, based on my own personal experiences. I encourage everyone to do the same when visiting a new country.

People have their own thoughts and assumptions about countries, their people, and places around the world. They base those thoughts on a combination of what they've digested in the media; heard from friends, family, or strangers; or endured themselves. No two travelers will have the same adventure. The best we can do is create our own view of a country based on our own experiences.

It's offensive when people judge the way I travel. Many assume they know what I have or haven't seen, heard, felt, or experienced. They truly have no idea. Rather than being so quick to judge, dissect, and express without knowing, go to that place and create your own experience. You can only ever have your own practical contact with others and observe events and facts of that place from your very own vantage point.

CHAPTER 12

FREEDOM TO LIVE AND A LEGACY LEFT BEHIND

You enter the force at the darkest point, where
there is no path. Where there is a way or path,
it is someone else's path. You are not on your
own path. If you follow someone else's way, you
are not going to realize your potential.

—JOSEPH CAMPBELL

The decade of time that I spent building, executing, and completing Expedition 196 came down to that one single moment in Yemen on February 2, 2017, when I stood at the threshold of victory. The anticipation, exhilaration, frustration, excitement, and sense of the unknown ran rapidly through my veins. I was about to finish this incredible journey I had undertaken. I had succeeded in leaving a positive legacy behind.

I look at my life as my own personal hero's journey, and I firmly believe everyone should do the same. Separation, initiation, and return are the three main stages of Joseph Campbell's *Hero's Journey*. During a time of my life when I felt desperate about both my personal life and my career, I had to make a decision to either continue down an ordinary path or to step outside myself and the regular life I was living into a world completely foreign to me. I had to decide whether being potentially misunderstood and strange to others was worth the risk I was about to undertake and endure.

I risked everything I had cultivated in my life up until that point and committed to Expedition 196. I wanted to come out the other side as the hero of my own life. I wanted to become a bullet ant. I made it my goal to make history, become an award-winning philanthropist and humanitarian, and a role model for young women to look up to in life.

In order to make my hero's journey, I had to sacrifice the things that make most humans' lives worthy, tolerable, and exciting. I had to let go of friendships, security, dating, social gatherings, sleep, simple pleasures, communication, comforts, wholesome meals, and most importantly, time. I had to give up aspects of myself and who I was, as well as to redefine what success meant to me.

In the quest for fulfillment, the journey to live authentically requires courage, strength, commitment, intestinal fortitude, and a thick skin. My quest to be fulfilled has been that of an entrepreneur.

Any entrepreneur who endures enough failures is in danger of getting to the point where they begin to expect a never-ending flow of losses. Having made the choice not to pin my career or success on others, I've always refused help, even when I needed it most. It's more important for me to be able to do things my way. Since the age of eighteen, my ethos has been to do what I want, when I want, and to inspire others along the way. Though I never had a specific vision of what my career would be exactly, from the place of child or young adult, I did know these things. It had to involve whatever I wanted, whenever I wanted, how I wanted to do it, and it had to inspire others.

I've endured unending harassment, unfair treatment from employers, and disappointing and upsetting experiences in the working world, which was severe and unforgiving at times. Life is a series of ups and downs, wins and losses, failures and successes.

The events of my life have taught me that most human beings experience some form of depression at one point or another in their life. For those of us who have had a chemical imbalance as long as we can remember, the word "fulfillment" becomes nebulous. In my opinion, no amount of money, success, or number of people assisted, will ever make me feel fulfilled. I see the world as a giant ball floating in a galaxy of the unknown, which makes me wonder if our ant lives are even worth the struggle or ups and downs it takes to survive.

Someone recently sent me a direct message on Instagram asking, "Did Expedition 196 make you feel fulfilled?" Up until that point, no one had asked me that before. If we're talking fulfillment in terms of simply achieving something desired or predicted, then yes. Expedition 196 did fulfill my desires—though only for a brief moment in time.

I achieved what I had set out to achieve, though the expedition didn't bring about my childhood dream in life because it wasn't what I dreamed it would be. Expedition 196 was merely a stepping stone to achieving the dream I remember as a child, which was to have my own show on the Travel Channel. I believed if I traveled a lot, in different ways, I would have so much to share with people on many places, cultures, and more on a show. When I was younger, I thought if I began at age twenty-one and finished traveling to every country in the world by age thirty, I'd get my own show and feel fulfilled in my career.

Unfortunately, even traveling to every sovereign nation on earth, making the type of life sacrifices I did, and risking my life, didn't get me what I really wanted. Had my hard work and sacrifices resulted in the television show I dreamed of having, I would feel fulfilled from the expedition in every way imaginable.

My early days of travel prior to the expedition allowed me creative freedom and the opportunity to explore the world and be nomadic. Expedition 196, on the other hand, was a career move, and an LLC that involved major work and investment. Expedition 196 was the most difficult emotionally, mentally, and physically taxing thing I've ever done in my life. Keeping my end goal in sight is what kept me going every step of the way.

Now that it's over, and I still haven't reached my career goal, I feel a significant void. I share this because it's how I truly feel about my accomplishments. I'm currently working on other plans and projects that will enable me to continue this career path of creative freedom and travel, though I fell short of my lifetime goal, and it's devastating. Whereas most people are okay even if they don't meet their career goals because they find a different type of satisfaction in getting married and having kids, but that's not for me. Neither of those things are a goal of mine. Career is the most important aspect of my life, and my focus remains 100 percent on this alone.

THE LEGACY

I put in many years of hard work with the hope of inspiring men and women alike. From where I sit today, it humbles me to realize that my dream to leave behind a positive legacy has become a reality.

It's important to clarify that my career isn't necessarily my legacy. While I would consider Expedition 196 my legacy for future generations of women in travel to aspire to, in their own lives, my personal legacy is Her International.

For whatever strange reason, I've never been able to visualize my life beyond age thirty. Instead of counting up, I've always counted down, as if some force of nature will snatch me up before my thirtieth year, which is why cultivating my legacy at such a young age has been important to me.

In October of 2017, I founded Her International, Inc. (www.her.international), the goal of which is to fund female-driven projects that address the United Nations Sustainable Development Goals. I was inspired to do this after nonprofit organizations denied my funding requests for Expedition 196 time and time again because I did not have a college degree. I never want a young woman or girl to feel limited based on their educational status. Her International is part of my legacy. Since I never want marriage or children, my legacy is my story, this book, and Her International, Inc.

As I sort through the dozens of applications I've received for Her International, Inc., I can't help but feel inspired by all the women who not only have a dream but who are taking actionable measures in order to make that dream a reality, as I did. It takes guts, courage, and commitment to bring a goal to life.

Now and then, I receive inspiring emails from women who have devoted themselves to break my record. It always makes me wonder why I chose to break this particular record rather than any one of the hundreds of travel records out there. Why did I feel the need to rush to and through every country when I could have enjoyed the journey? I know.

As a woman, I saw an opportunity to do something that had only been achieved by a man. To break through those barriers and make women's history was an obvious choice. I don't like to think I am limited in life because of my gender. I have an innate desire to prove to the world that the seemingly impossible is, in fact, possible. It can be done. And I did it. I proved that a woman can not only shatter a man's record but that she can travel far and wide alone.

I wonder why so many of my fellow females want to break my record rather than breaking through the glass ceiling by going for the records that only men have achieved to date. Perhaps it's just to prove that if it can be done once, it can be done again. The problem is that, as this record continues to be broken, travelers will see and experience less and less each time.

To anyone who wants to break this record for the sake of fame and fortune, I encourage you to think long and hard about what you want your own legacy to be.

To me, this record was a legacy since I was the first female to accomplish it. Also, it was a stepping stone to my ultimate career goal. I hope that women who break my record also use it as a stepping stone to a greater destiny, since sacrificing so much to travel so quickly is hardly fulfilling.

Travel in the more general sense, should be an enjoyable and educational journey rather than a rush and a risk—unless, of course, there is history to be made. By sacrificing my own ability to fully experience each country the way I'd have liked to do, I hoped to pave the way for women who aspire to explore corners of the world alone and feel they can do it safely.

IN THE END, WE'RE ALL THE SAME

I hope you walk away from this book inspired to pursue your own legacy, regardless of what anyone tells you that you can or cannot do in life. I hope my story opens your eyes to the struggles and celebrations we all experience in life. And I hope it inspires you to be kind to someone because you never know the struggles they might be facing.

More than a decade after that stormy night in the little New England town of Litchfield, I've done everything in my power to abide by the promise I made to myself to never be low income again. However, in that time, I've also learned that in order to continue to inspire, there comes a time when you must let go of your own selfish needs and devote your life to the livelihood of others.

Every single person on this planet has a story, and every one of us has suffered at one point or another. The way we treat one another online and in person can make or break a life. Hatred and degradation never gets easier, especially for those of us in the public eye. Each and every human in this world has the right to live and breathe according to the beat of their own heart, as long as they aren't harming others in the process. Each of us is just trying to survive and to live life the best that we possibly can. Be a little bit easier on people you don't know. Assume they're going through the worst and are hiding their emotions behind a heavy, opaque red velvet curtain.

If there's one thing all humans have in common, it's that we're all the result of biology and evolution. Every single day, I think of myself as an ant. Many days, it's hard for me to care about what seems like little matters of politics, religion, and global events when I exist on a comparatively small orb in this endless galaxy. For all of us, the cycle of life is relatively quick and meaningless in relation to the vastness of time. In a moment, we are born, live a full life, and then die. Each year, 131 million human beings are born and 55 million of us die. Year after year, birth and death. Year after year, this orb we live on circles round, and year after year, we face the uncertainty that comes from not knowing when it will all come to an end.

After traveling to every country in the world and witnessing various life forms, no matter how good, successful, pretty, or cool a person is or thinks they are, each of us is just the same. We are all perishable and mortal, made of a cocktail of compound elements. We are equal in that we each go through the same process of biological life only to disintegrate back into the elements from which we're made.

So what's it all worth? And can anyone ever really be fulfilled? Can anyone be truly happy or satisfied? Even as someone who has traveled to 196 countries on earth, what I've seen is so small compared to the vastness of space. I have not seen the depths of our earth's core nor journeyed out into the galaxy through which we float. Until I see those two things, I don't think I'll ever feel fulfilled.

Ask yourself, what type of ant are you? And what type of ant do you want to be? What will it take for you to make such a profound impact on our world that it can be felt from outer space?

Or perhaps you don't care to be seen from space, and that's okay too.

The most effective way to do it, is to do it.

— AMELIA EARHART

ACKNOWLEDGMENTS

To mom and dad, without whose undeniable support and sacrifice I would not be here. My victories are yours. Jason, my blood brother, whose sound and level-headed advice got me through the most difficult of times. A sincere thank you to the undying love of sweet Kishmere, Noah, Kiku, Piper, and Sophie, because cats and dogs are the most healing of creatures to come home to after years away. Thank you, Janelle, my other half, who stood by my side through the most difficult and successful of times, no matter what. I thank you for being the one friend who I can trust to take anywhere with me on an epic adventure. Thank you, Christopher, for providing your undeniable support and distant connection in the most depressive of times. You were the one person who I could relate to with each experience I had in every country in the world.

Louis D'Amore from the International Institute of Peace Through Tourism and Nigel Pilkington of Skål International, I am forever indebted to your immense resources, connections, and understanding as I grew from a naive backpacker to a professional in the travel industry. You introduced me to thousands of university and high school students around the world, as well as mayors, ministers of tourism, and Nandi Mandela (Nelson Mandela's granddaughter), Naomi King (Martin Luther King Jr.'s sister-in-law), and the king of Spain, among many others, and you gave me the most pleasurable opportunity to plant trees around the world to offset my carbon footprint from the expedition. Also, thank you to Adventure Scientists for giving me the opportunity to volunteer for your organization, collecting water samples around the world to test for the presence of micro plastics. Thank you to David of World Travel and Tourism (WTTC) for introducing me to the best in the travel industry.

To my supporters: Paul Liberstein ("Toby" from NBC's *The Office*), Sebastian Copeland (filmmaker and author of *Into the Cold*), and Ranulph Fiennes (multiple Guinness World Record breaker and "World's Greatest Living Explorer"), you all made me sound believable in my early stages, and I thank you for your support.

To my sponsors, specifically Rhonda and Jeff at AIG Travel, thank you for believing in me and providing kidnap and ransom insurance, you had my back from the very beginning and were, and still are, a lifesaving company that I have the honor of working with. Matt, Jason, AJ, and the rest of the kick-ass team at Krav Maga Worldwide for teaching me how to defend myself in the worst of situations. To the team of Quark Expeditions, for allowing me to experience my last and final continent: Antarctica. And to all my sponsors and investors who made Expedition 196 possible: Air New Zealand, Avianca, Clif Bar, Dogeared, Eagle Creek, Soneva, Six Senses, and all who have contributed in the form of cash, goods, and services, you got me through to the finish line.

To all the fascinating and hospitable human beings from every country in the world who I've had the pleasure of connecting with, I owe my positive outlook of this world to you.

And thank you to my virtual supporters who have stuck with me throughout my life's journey since *Naked and Afraid*. Your continuing support and positivity is what drives me to continue creating worthy and exhilarating content and material.

Lastly, I want to thank my good health that I've been able to maintain through fitness and healthy food consumption that enabled me to keep going and stay sane throughout this whole thing. Health is wealth, and I firmly believe in that.

ABOUT THE AUTHOR

CASSIE DE PECOL is the first woman on record to travel to every country in the world; a two-time Guinness World Record holder; CEO of Expedition 196, LLC; and Founder of Her International, Inc. She is considered the world's most prolific traveler of her time, exemplifying cause-driven sophistication and passion through her travels. A keynote speaker, brand ambassador, Ironman athlete, author, and content creator, Cassie's career has just begun. To learn more, visit her website (www.cassiedepecol.com) and the website for Her International, Inc. (www.her.international).

FOLLOW CASSIE:

Instagram: @cassiedepecol
Facebook: facebook.com/cassiedepecol
Twitter: @cassiedepecol
YouTube: youtube.com/c/cassiedepecol

CPSIA information can be obtained
at www.ICGtesting.com
Printed in the USA
LVHW01*0350310718
585355LV00014B/394/P